THE MACMI

KU-351-145

ADVISORY EDITO
Professor of English, University of York

GENERAL EDITOR: PETER HOLLINDALE
Senior Lecturer in English and Education, University of York

THE TEMPEST

Other titles in the series:

THE MACMILLAN SHAKESPEARE

THE TEMPEST

Edited by
A. C. and J. E. Spearing

M
Macmillan Education

First published 1971
Reprinted 1975, 1977

Published by
MACMILLAN EDUCATION LTD
*Houndmills Basingstoke Hampshire RG21 2XS
and London*

*Associated companies in Delhi Dublin
Hong Kong Johannesburg Lagos Melbourne
New York Singapore and Tokyo*

Printed in Great Britain by
RICHARD CLAY (THE CHAUCER PRESS) LTD
Bungay, Suffolk

CONTENTS

INTRODUCTION

I: *THE DATE AND TEXT OF THE TEMPEST*

The first recorded production of *The Tempest* took place on 1 November 1611, when it was performed before King James I at Whitehall by the King's Men – the company of actors in which Shakespeare was a member and shareholder. There is no reason to suppose that this was the play's first night: it may well have been performed before this to the public at the Globe or the Blackfriars, both theatres belonging to the King's Men. But it is likely that the writing of the play was completed in the same year as this performance. The chief reason for supposing this is that Shakespeare in composing *The Tempest* seems to have made use of certain pamphlets describing a shipwreck in the Bermudas, and the first of these was not written until late in 1610. So we can say fairly definitely that *The Tempest* dates from 1611.

It was performed again at Court two winters later. It was one of several plays, including others by Shakespeare, put on to celebrate the visit of the Elector Palatine, a German prince who was visiting England in order to marry King James's daughter Elizabeth. It is clear that the masque in Act IV of *The Tempest* would be particularly suitable for performance on the occasion of a wedding or, still more, of an engagement, because that is the purpose it serves within the play. Moreover, within the play, the couple for whose benefit the masque is devised are, like the Elector and Elizabeth, a prince and princess. All this has led many scholars to argue that the masque must have been specially added to *The Tempest* for this second Court performance, so that the first Court performance would have been of a different version of the play, now lost. But the evidence will scarcely prove this. Shakespeare's comedies tend to direct themselves towards the marriages of princes and princesses, and it is easy to suppose that *The Tempest* was chosen for performance before the Elector and the Princess simply as a successful play that happened to be vaguely appropriate to the occasion. In any case, even if there was an earlier version of *The Tempest*, we know nothing of it, and can only concentrate on the play we have. It is worth our study.

The Tempest was first published in the earliest collected edition of Shakespeare's plays, known as the 'First Folio', put together in 1623 by two of his fellow-actors, seven years after his death. It is the first play in the collection, and shows signs of having been treated with great care by the editors. The Folio text is carefully punctuated; unlike many of the plays in the collection, it is divided into acts and scenes and given a list of characters, including brief descriptions of some of the parts ('an honest old Councillor', 'an airy spirit', and so on); above all, it is supplied with some very elaborate stage directions, describing the stage-picture and sound-effects as they might have appeared in an actual production. There is reason to suppose that these stage directions are closely based on Shakespeare's own, though we have them not in their original theatrical form (as instructions to the stage manager) but in a more descriptive literary form. The directions – for example, those in Act three, scene 3 – are often an essential part of the text of the play, and in this edition we have treated them as such. They are often poetically suggestive in their wording, and they help to give a sense of the lavishness with which the play was probably staged in the Banqueting House at Whitehall, where elaborate scenery and stage-machinery were available.

II: *THE SOURCES OF THE TEMPEST*

Like nearly all great writers before the eighteenth century, Shakespeare was not in the habit of inventing his own stories: he preferred to rework already existing material. There are only three of Shakespeare's plays for whose stories some definite source cannot be found in romance, chronicle, or folktale. One of these is *The Tempest*. No certain source has ever been discovered for the main narrative of the events on Prospero's island. Scholars have pointed to various similarities between Shakespeare's story and those of certain German and Spanish works of the sixteenth century, all of which feature a ruler-magician who, like Prospero, withdraws from the everyday world and takes his daughter with him. But the similarities are not close enough for us to think of any of these works as actual sources for the play as a whole.

Some interesting sources have been discovered, however, for certain parts of the play. Prospero's island is in the Mediterranean, but the Bermudas are once mentioned by Ariel; and it seems extremely likely that Shakespeare's imagination was stimulated by accounts of a particular shipwreck in the Bermudas. These are contained in three pamphlets written in 1610: *A True Reportory of the Wrack and Redemption of Sir Thomas Gates* by William Strachey (whom Shakespeare may have known personally); *A Discovery of the Bermudas* by Silvester Jourdain; and *The True Declaration of the Estate of the Colony in Virginia*, an official account of the matter published by the Council of Virginia (which was then a British colony).[1] All three recount how a fleet of ships carrying colonists to Virginia was attacked by a terrible storm, which separated the *Sea Adventure*, containing the expedition's leaders, Sir Thomas Gates and Sir George Somers, from the others.

[1] Shakespeare's use of these pamphlets has been studied by Morton Luce, in his edition of *The Tempest* (1901); R. R. Cawley, 'Shakespeare's Use of the Voyagers', *Publications of the Modern Language Association of America* XLI (1926); and J. P. Brockbank, '*The Tempest*: Conventions of Art and Empire' in *Shakespeare's Last Plays*, ed. J. R. Brown and B. Harris (1966). The texts of the pamphlets are easily available in L. G. Wright, *The Elizabethans' America* (1966), from which we here quote them. Incidentally, Shakespeare uses the language of seamanship with some technical skill, and we have found great help in interpreting parts of *The Tempest* in two books by A. F. Falconer, *Shakespeare and the Sea* (1964) and *A Glossary of Shakespeare's Sea and Naval Terms* (1965).

3

The *Sea Adventure* was battered by the storm for four days on end until, just when the voyagers were giving up hope, Somers sighted land, and they managed to run the ship aground off the Bermudas. All the voyagers and much of the cargo were saved, and they found the Bermudas far more comfortable than their contemporary name of 'the Devil's Islands' would have suggested. They eventually reached Virginia, and there Gates, the governor, found that mutinies had broken out in his absence. Shakespeare found much to interest him in this story of storm, shipwreck, and rebellion. Strachey gives a vivid description of the storm, as the voyagers themselves experienced it, and tells how 'their clamours drowned in the winds, and the winds in thunder'. This clearly leaves its mark in the confusion portrayed in the opening scene of the play. Strachey also describes St Elmo's fire, in the form of which Ariel says he appeared (I. 2. 196–8). Jourdain adds the detail of how the voyagers drank to each other when they thought they were about to drown (compare the Boatswain's 'What, must our mouths be cold?' [I. 1. 53]). He also emphasises the wonder felt by the voyagers at their unexpected preservation, a feeling that appears prominently in *The Tempest*. The Bermudas were thought of as 'a most prodigious and enchanted place' – certainly not the holiday resort they are now – and, Jourdain writes, 'our delivery was not more strange, in falling so opportunely and happily upon the land, as our feeding and preservation was beyond our hopes and all men's expectations most admirable'. All three pamphlets give a powerful emphasis to the part played by Divine Providence and Divine Mercy in bringing about the voyagers' salvation, and this too is a recurrent feeling in the play, aroused both by the survival of the royal party and by the earlier survival of Prospero and Miranda. The pamphleteers unquestioningly see the shipwreck not simply as a physical ordeal but as having a moral and spiritual meaning: the very word 'Redemption' in Strachey's title suggests how

4

far this extends. The *True Declaration* in particular takes the external dangers of sea and storm as natural symbols of men's inner experience, and writes of the 'gulf of despair' into which the voyagers fell and the 'tempest of dissension' that awaited them in Virginia. There is just this kind of intimate connection between the physical and the moral in the play: there too 'tempest' and 'dissension' reflect each other. The *True Declaration* even sees the events in theatrical terms, as forming a 'tragical comedy'. In these pamphlets the stage was already set for Shakespeare's play.

We are not suggesting, however, that Shakespeare would have been unable to arrive at such ideas if he had not happened to read the pamphlets. The dependence is not of that kind: it is rather that Shakespeare found in the pamphlets powerful reinforcement for ways of seeing life that were already present in his drama. Partly because much of the early colonisation of North America was carried out by men fleeing from religious persecution, the literature of voyages and colonisation is pervaded with a sense of spiritual meaning: the New World offers a 'new life'. And this theme of human renewal through a merciful Providence had already been developed by Shakespeare in others of his later comedies. In *The Tempest* he does not share the naïvety of the pamphleteers: the 'brave new world' that Miranda exclaims over is, ironically, the old world after all, the world of Italy with all its ingrained sins, and Prospero must add the reservation, ''Tis new to thee'.

Closely connected with the Bermuda pamphlets is another source for *The Tempest*: the essay *Of the Cannibals* by the French moralist Michel de Montaigne. Montaigne's essays had been published in an English translation in 1603, and Shakespeare certainly knew them. Montaigne writes of the American Indians as having established an ideal society of exactly the kind imagined by Gonzalo in Act two, scene 1, and he contrasts the innocent perfection of their natural life with the corruptions due to human art in supposedly civilised society. The contrast between Nature and Art runs throughout *The Tempest*. Nature at its lowest is represented by Caliban, whose very name suggests cannibal; Art at its highest by the magical and moral 'Art' of Prospero. The contrast between Art (or Nurture) and Nature was a common one in Renaissance thought; and we cannot say that Shakespeare was merely following Montaigne's opinions, for Montaigne's idealism about Nature could scarcely accommodate the half-bestial Caliban. However, if Caliban is half a beast, and even part devil, a 'thing of darkness' (V. I. 275), he also has traces of nobility, and the contrast between his poetic perceptiveness and the total debasement of Stephano and Trinculo, those dregs of civilisation, is very much along Montaigne's lines.

Finally we must mention one other possible source, this time for the part of the story told in retrospect by Prospero in Act one, scene 2. For this tale of callous usurpation, Shakespeare could have found a number of hints in Thomas's *History of Italy*, published in 1549.[1] In Shakespeare's time Italy was divided into a large number of small states, whose alliances and enmities changed with great rapidity. It is from this historical Italy that the human characters of the play have come to the enchanted island. In Thomas, connected with confused stories of usurpation and banishment in Milan and Naples, Shakespeare could have found the names Prospero (meaning in Latin 'I cause to succeed,' and therefore beautifully suggestive of the character's part in the play), Ferdinand, and Anthonio.

What above all Shakespeare seems to have found in the sources mentioned is not a plot for his play so much as suggestive groupings of ideas and feelings – a fruitful soil out of which a play might grow.

[1] See J. M. Nosworthy, 'The Narrative Sources of *The Tempest*' in *Review of English Studies* XXIV (1948).

6

III: *THE PLACE OF THE TEMPEST IN SHAKE-SPEARE'S WORK*

The Tempest is the last play which we can be sure was written wholly by Shakespeare. In the later stages of his career he seems to have been in the habit of collaborating with younger dramatists who also wrote for the King's Men, such as John Fletcher. The plays *Pericles* (1608–9), *Henry VIII* (1612–13) and *The Two Noble Kinsmen* (1613) are generally thought to be the products of such collaboration. Despite this, Shakespeare critics from the later nineteenth century onwards have been in agreement that his last four or five plays – *Pericles* and *Henry VIII* (so far as they are his) *Cymbeline* (1609–10), *The Winter's Tale* (1610–11), and *The Tempest* – form a closely linked group, having more in common than any other group of his plays, and throwing much light on each other. As early as 1904, Lytton Strachey noted how they shared a violence of expression, 'unreality' of atmosphere, and improbability of plotting, qualities which he found in particular concentration in *The Tempest*.[1] But Strachey, in common with earlier critics, inclined to see this group of plays in biographical terms, as directly expressing the supposed boredom and weariness of an ageing playwright. More recent critics, nearly all strongly influenced by the important work of G. Wilson Knight,[2] have tended to see the last plays as symbolic dramas which form the culminating development of Shakespeare's career as a dramatist and of his vision of life, without necessarily reflecting his psychological state in any direct way. The stories of all the last plays but *Henry VIII* have striking similarities: they concern the separation and reunion of royal parents and their children; the reunions are seen as something more than

[1] 'Shakespeare's Final Period', reprinted in *Books and Characters* (1906).
[2] Especially *The Shakespearian Tempest* (1932) and *The Crown of Life* (1947). Wilson Knight's views early received the weighty support of T. S. Eliot (see his essay of 1932, 'John Ford').

7

natural, brought about by a force which is in some sense regenerative or redemptive; and in *Pericles*, *The Winter's Tale*, and *The Tempest* the sea has great symbolic importance, as a power at once terrible and mysteriously merciful. Wilson Knight has shown how these themes develop out of and complete the preoccupations of Shakespeare's great tragedies. 'Tragedy is never the last word,' Wilson Knight has remarked, and he sees the last plays as 'myths of immortality' which take us into a religious joy on the far side of the tragic experience. Thus Leontes in *The Winter's Tale* suffers from a jealousy as intense as Othello's and so enters a world of nightmare as delirious as Macbeth's, while in *The Tempest* the plot against Alonso's life once more offers a 'striking recapitulation of *Macbeth*'. Both plays, however, end not with death but with redemption and the renewal of life in a younger generation. Moreover, the very storm after which *The Tempest* is named has been a powerful symbol of natural and moral disaster in the great tragedies; now it lies within the control of providential magic. In the tragedies and last plays alike, storm and music are opposed as symbols of disorder and of healing calm; and this is clearly of great importance for our understanding of the songs and other music of *The Tempest*. E. M. W. Tillyard, too, has argued that the last plays take a stage further processes of regeneration and renewal that began in the tragedies.[1]

Criticism since the middle of this century has noticed in the last plays a further element: a certain theatricality, not the result of accident or incompetence, but of conscious art.[2] In all of these plays, an emphasis on spectacle and an unconcealed manipulation of tension produce a sense

[1] *Shakespeare's Last Plays* (1938).
[2] For example: S. L. Bethell, *The Winter's Tale: a Study* (1947); J. P. Brockbank, 'History and Histrionics in *Cymbeline*', *Shakespeare Survey* XI (1958); Leslie Fiedler, 'Shakespeare and the Paradox of Illusion' in *No! in Thunder* (1963).

that what we are watching is admittedly a *play*, which is not pretending to create the illusion of real life. This theatrical quality of the last plays may arise partly from the fact that Shakespeare was now writing for a new theatre. In 1608 the King's Men had acquired the Blackfriars Theatre, an indoor playhouse, smaller than the outdoor Globe, and more exclusive in its audiences. It may well have encouraged the development of a more technically sophisticated and self-aware drama.[1] Certainly, in the last plays we are much more conscious than in the great tragedies of the formal characteristics of drama. Both *Pericles* and *The Winter's Tale* have Choruses, who comment on the structures of the plays as they are unfolded. And *The Winter's Tale* and *The Tempest* seem to be deliberately contrived as examples of extreme opposites in dramatic structure. *The Winter's Tale* has scenes that range from one country to another and over a huge period of time, with a gap of sixteen years in the middle being blandly excused by the Chorus. The action of *The Tempest*, on the other hand, takes place on a single island, and is compressed into a period of three hours – approximately the same time as the play takes to perform. It conforms so perfectly to the 'rules' that the literary theorists of Shakespeare's time derived from Aristotle and Horace that it must surely have been intended for an audience who would appreciate its classical perfection. Consider particularly Act one, scene 2. Here all the past events we need to know about are summarised in an exposition of almost showy skill. We cannot fail to notice how clever Shakespeare is being in thus concentrating the whole relevant past into a plausibly motivated narrative; yet he seems almost to be mocking his own cleverness, by making Miranda so sleepy, and Prospero so anxious that

[1] See G. E. Bentley, 'Shakespeare and the Blackfriars Theatre', in *Shakespeare Survey* I (1948). It must not be forgotten, however, that some of the last plays were also performed at the Globe.

9

she should take in every word. One result of this device is to create a feeling of great urgency, for if Prospero does not seize his opportunity on this crucial afternoon his 'fortunes will ever after droop' (I. 2. 183-4). Another result is to keep us aware that it is a play we are watching, a work of human art, not a slice of life.

A further influence on the theatrical and spectacular effects in the last plays, and particularly in *The Tempest*, was the growing taste in the early seventeenth century for masques.[1] These were shows, combining elements of pageant, ballet, and opera, in which some symbolic action was presented through poetry, music, dancing, and elaborate scenic effects. They were, we may say, elegant pantomimes for adults; and the Blackfriars had been famous for them before the King's Men took it over. *The Tempest* includes a masque, devised by Prospero to entertain Ferdinand and Miranda, but there is also much that is masque-like about the play as a whole. Just as in masques, the play's goal is achieved by disclosure or revelation rather than by dramatic conflict and uncertainty. The chief dramatic events of the story have already taken place when the play opens; the original usurpation of Prospero is not enacted, but is merely reflected in the two plots against him on the island, which remain under his control. On the other hand, he is inside the play, not a mere Chorus commenting on it from the outside, and the real drama of *The Tempest* goes on within Prospero's mind – in his struggle against his own anger, resentment, desire for vengeance, and even forgetfulness. It is significant that the masque of Juno and Ceres is not allowed to reach a serenely predictable conclusion, but is abruptly broken off by Prospero under the influence of 'some passion that works him strongly' (IV. 1. 143-4).

In creating works of this kind in his last plays, Shakespeare was not merely following a fashion for something new. Wilson Knight and Northrop Frye have reminded us

[1] See Enid Welsford, *The Court Masque* (1927).

that he was also going back to a kind of drama he had produced earlier in his career, and giving a final turn to its meaning.[1] Among Shakespeare's earlier plays are some half-dozen romantic comedies, plays whose stories were usually taken from prose romances of a kind that retained their popularity throughout his life.[2] As an example of these we may take *As You Like It*, a play in which the following events (among others) occur. A good duke is usurped by his younger brother (Frederick) and flees to live in the forest. Frederick's cruelty drives both the good duke's daughter (Rosalind) and his own to flee to the forest too. The man with whom Rosalind has fallen in love also flees to the forest, driven there by the cruelty of *his* brother (Oliver). Both the wicked brothers are converted to goodness, Frederick by meeting an 'old religious man', and Oliver by being saved from a lion by his banished brother. Eventually all ends well, except that one lord attending on the good duke cannot be reconciled, and the play concludes with a masque celebrating marriage and an epilogue addressed by Rosalind to the audience. When we add that Rosalind, who brings about the happy ending, has claimed to have the help of 'a magician, most profound in his art, and yet not damnable,' it will become clear that *As You Like It* has many similarities with *The Tempest*: the good duke banished by his usurping brother to a 'natural' or 'desert' setting, far from civilisation; the triumph of love and forgiveness; the not-quite-complete reconciliation and return to the civilised world; the hints of religion and white magic; the masque and the epilogue. However, themes and motifs of this kind may be given greater or lesser significance, according to the way the dramatist treats them. In *As You Like It*, on the whole,

[1] Northrop Frye, 'The Argument of Comedy', reprinted in *Shakespeare's Comedies: an Anthology of Modern Criticism*, ed. Laurence Lerner (1967); and *A Natural Perspective* (1965).

[2] See Tillyard, and also E. C. Pettet, *Shakespeare and the Romance Tradition* (1949) and J. F. Danby, *Poets on Fortune's Hill* (1952) (reprinted as *Elizabethan and Jacobean Poets*).

they are used to make up a fairy tale, offering a pleasant escape from real life, and little more; though it must be added that, even in this early play, there is witty discussion of Art and Nature, and frequent reminders that our wishes for the final happiness of the characters can be fulfilled only in play. It is art, not life, that produces a world 'as we like it'. These more serious implications of romantic comedy are brought out far more fully in *The Tempest* than in any of Shakespeare's early comedies. In order to be brought out, they require not only the dramatist's mature thought but also his mature poetry; and in the richness, complexity, and intensity of its poetry *The Tempest* does not merely excel the early comedies but stands, with *The Winter's Tale*, as the greatest work of Shakespeare's final phase. The help that twentieth-century critics have given us by bringing out the similarities of the last plays must not be used to blur the differences in *quality* within this group of works. The same thematic materials may be used in all of them, but they are organised now more, now less, coherently, and express significances now more, now less, profound.[1] Among them *The Tempest*, with its combination of diversity and control, intensity and subtlety, is in our view the greatest.

IV: *THE PLAY*

The opening scene of *The Tempest* is one of startlingly violent realism. Without warning, we are plunged into the fury and confusion of a storm at sea, in which the shouts of the agitated passengers and crew have to make themselves heard against 'a tempestuous noise of thunder and lightning' and the shrilling of the Master's whistle. And those are all the devices Shakespeare uses. Where the modern stage would employ elaborate lighting and perhaps even cinematic effects, Shakespeare, even at Whitehall or

[1] This point has been made by F. R. Leavis in his essay 'The Criticism of Shakespeare's Late Plays', reprinted in *The Common Pursuit* (1952).

the Blackfriars, relied mainly on human and other sounds – sounds which can evoke the scene for us today with extraordinary vividness, even if we have never seen it performed.

All the rest of the play takes place on Prospero's island, an enchanted world which is in many ways utterly different from the 'real' world of the first scene. To the shipwrecked party it seems that they have been transported into a fairytale. The experiences they undergo on the island are felt by them to be strange, wonderful, unnatural – these are words that echo throughout the play. It is full of images of sleep and dreaming, and many of the things that happen are dreamlike, or nightmarish: songs and voices coming from nowhere, mysteriously appearing and disappearing banquets and masques, and above all perhaps that sensation, so common in nightmares, of desperately needing to take action and yet finding oneself paralysed. This happens to Ferdinand when he draws his sword to respond to Prospero's threats – 'My spirits, as in a dream, are all bound up' (I. 2. 489) – and it happens again to Alonso, Anthonio, and Sebastian when they draw their swords against Ariel. Again, the voyagers see their experiences as being like the strange tales told by travellers of unicorns and phoenixes (III. 3. 21–4). They grasp at various possible explanations of these experiences. One is that they are caused by the gods, or by God – the play's theology is deliberately vague. Ferdinand, when he first sees Miranda, assumes that she must be a goddess. Alonso's reaction is the same:

> Is she the goddess that hath severed us,
> And brought us thus together? (V. 1. 187–8)

But by now Ferdinand is able to correct him. The evil members of the royal party are more inclined to see the island's strangeness as the work of devils, an explanation that no doubt reflects their own natures. After the apparitions of Act three, scene 3, Sebastian cries out:

But one fiend at a time,
I'll fight their legions o'er.   (III. 3. 102–3)

This is his reaction again in the final scene, when he discovers that Prospero mysteriously knows of his wickedness: 'The Devil speaks in him' (V. 1. 129). But Prospero immediately gives an authoritative 'No'. In the same scene, the wonder of the voyagers reaches its climax. Even Sebastian goes on to see what has happened as 'a most high miracle' (177), and Alonso is convinced that some supernatural power has been at work:

These are not natural events, they strengthen
From strange to stranger . . .

This is as strange a maze as e'er men trod,
And there is in this business more than nature
Was ever conduct of.   (227–8, 242–4)

This sense of strangeness, then, pervades the play from its second scene to its last. But it is striking that we see the strange events not only through the wondering glances of the voyagers, but also through Prospero's informed eyes. The first scene on the island is largely devoted to giving an explanation of Prospero's and Miranda's presence there, his magical powers, and the two strange servants they have enabled him to acquire. This explanation is given almost entirely in natural, not supernatural terms. As everywhere in the play, there are occasional suggestions that 'Providence divine' played its part (I. 2. 159), but in general Prospero's explanation belongs to the world of men, not that of fairytale or miracle. A modern reader might protest that magic itself inevitably belongs to the world of fairytale; but in Shakespeare's time this was not so. Then it was still possible to believe in magic, and to see it as a branch of science. King James I himself believed in witches and magic, and he was one of the most learned of English kings. In *The Tempest* Shakespeare takes great care to integrate Prospero's magical powers with the realistic political story that is told in the second scene. Prospero acquired his special powers gradually, by a long process of study, and it was precisely the seclusion this made necessary that gave his brother the opportunity and the incentive to take his place. Care is taken, too, to identify Prospero's magic as natural, or white, not black. His power derives not from the aid of devils, but, like the scientist's, from observation of and co-operation with natural phenomena. Only in the great soliloquy of Act five does he seem to go beyond this, when he claims that

> graves at my command
> Have waked their sleepers, oped, and let 'em forth
> By my so potent Art.   (V. 1. 48–50)

Even such miracles are now coming to seem within the grasp of science; and in general, as the Polish critic Jan Kott has emphasised,[1] this great speech describes a power which is essentially scientific. In Shakespeare's time, indeed, it was only a dream; now it is the terrible reality of nuclear physics, which has truly

> bedimmed
> The noontide sun, called forth the mutinous winds,
> And 'twixt the green sea and the azured vault
> Set roaring war.   (V. 1. 41–4)

Even Prospero's two strange servants, Caliban and Ariel, are treated realistically as far as possible. Given an initial belief, such as men in Shakespeare's time had, in the possible existence of 'airy spirits' and of wild men halfway between human beings and animals, we should find nothing implausible in their introduction. Like Prospero's magic, both are given carefully drawn backgrounds in Act one, scene 2. Prospero is given an excuse

[1] *Shakespeare Our Contemporary* (1965). This book contains an extremely stimulating chapter on *The Tempest*.

to repeat how Ariel was punished by Caliban's mother, the witch Sycorax, and how her death left Caliban master of the island and Ariel imprisoned, until Prospero arrived. Prospero came to the island as a colonist, like those of the Bermuda pamphlets; and the apparent fantasy of Caliban is grounded in the reality of Shakespeare's time. He is one version – a sombre one – of the stories of the native inhabitants of the Americas brought back by the first European colonisers. Moreover, with a creative power that has long been admired, Shakespeare has supplied both Caliban and Ariel with a kind of language and behaviour that exactly fits their imaginary histories. The poet John Dryden's praise of Caliban's realism, written in 1679, is so apt that it is worth quoting here:

> The poet has most judiciously furnished him with a person, a language, and a character, which will suit him, both by father's and mother's side: he has all the discontents and malice of a witch, and of a devil, besides a convenient proportion of the deadly sins; gluttony, sloth, and lust are manifest; the dejectedness of a slave is likewise given him, and the ignorance of one bred up in a desert island. His person is monstrous, as he is the product of unnatural lust; and his language is as hobgoblin as his person.[1]

This 'hobgoblin' language has its nose, like a dog's, to the ground, is thickly sown with the names of solid things, and presents every thought not as an idea but a reality. Thus the human villain Anthonio speaks of killing as 'laying to bed for ever' or 'putting to the perpetual wink' (II. 2. 285–6); but Caliban, less squeamishly, says

> thou mayst brain him,
> Having first seized his books; or with a log
> Batter his skull, or paunch him with a stake,
> Or cut his wezand with thy knife.   (III. 2. 90–3)

[1] From Dryden's *Preface to Troilus and Cressida*. By *convenient* Dryden means 'appropriate'.

Yet this very tendency to experience thoughts as concrete realities is capable of arousing pity, as when Caliban speaks like a child of how

> in dreaming,
> The clouds methought would open, and show riches
> Ready to drop upon me, that when I waked
> I cried to dream again.   (III. 2. 142–5)

It is easy to understand how, at first, Prospero and Miranda stroked Caliban and made much of him (I. 2. 334); but he is repeatedly compared to a fish, in a way that makes him sound repellently slimy, smelly, and cold-blooded. Perhaps in performance there might be suggestions of fins as well as fur in his costume. In the case of Ariel, the equivalent suggestions would be of feathers; he is repeatedly referred to as a bird. He is a more purely fantastic figure, with little of the human about him, but he too is given a distinctive language of his own, delicate and musical, remote from the earth. His great desire is not, like Caliban's, for material things – food, wealth, power, sex – but simply for freedom.

Ariel and Caliban have important parts to play in the serious meaning of *The Tempest*. It is, on one level, a play about forgiveness.[1] Ariel's role is to provoke forgiveness in Prospero, while Caliban's is to be incapable of being forgiven. Because Ariel is not even partly human, he has a kind of detachment, an innocent cruelty, in the task he is set of tormenting the royal party: he is more aware of his own ingenuity than of their suffering. But at last he does come to be aware of their suffering, and even to have an inkling of what human pity for them might be like:

> *Ariel*   Your charm so strongly works 'em
> That, if you now beheld them, your affections
> Would become tender.

[1] This is emphasised by R. G. Hunter, *Shakespeare and the Comedy of Forgiveness* (1965).

17

> *Prospero*   Dost thou think so, spirit?
> *Ariel* Mine would, sir, were I human.   (V. 1. 17–20)

This insight of Ariel's marks a turning-point for Prospero. If even Ariel, who is 'but air', can feel compassion for the suffering voyagers, so will he, and he decides to take the part of 'virtue' rather than 'vengeance'. Caliban, on the other hand, has rejected all the attempts of Prospero and Miranda to civilise him. We may be tempted to feel sympathy for him, as a native cruelly exploited and enslaved by colonists, but the savage malice of his acts and utterances will not allow us to forget that he is something less than human –

> A devil, a born devil, on whose nature
> Nurture can never stick.   (IV. 1. 188–9)

Anthonio and Sebastian may be forgiven, but not Caliban. At the end of the play, when the human characters sail back into civilisation, Caliban alone remains behind on the island, unreconciled, and once more 'his own king' (I. 2. 343). But at the very end there is just a hint that eventually he too may be capable of reform and thus of forgiveness:

> I'll be wise hereafter,
> And seek for grace.   (V. 1. 295–6)

It appears, then, that the supernatural and fantastic elements in *The Tempest*, are not simply, as they were in earlier comedies such as *As You Like It*, facts outside the play mentioned solely in order to bring about a happy ending. They are a central part of the play, have a serious meaning, and are treated, as far as may be, realistically. It is true that a number of nineteenth- and twentieth-century critics have tended to see these elements in allegorical terms[1] – to see Ariel, for instance, as standing

---

[1] Such attempts are discussed by A. D. Nuttall in his excellent book *Two Concepts of Allegory* (1967), which is mainly con-

for the poetic inspiration. But there seems to be no limit to such interpretations, no way of distinguishing allegorical meanings in the play from those in the critic's mind; and to translate a complex and richly suggestive human drama into a rigid pattern of abstractions is to risk failing to confront the experience at the heart of the play at all. This experience is largely one of suffering, caused by the supernatural means we have been discussing. There is repeated throughout the play a single definition of what is happening to the royal party: they are, in a quite literal sense, going mad. The opening storm pushes all the voyagers over the brink of sanity, as Ariel explains:

> Not a soul
> But felt a fever of the mad, and played
> Some tricks of desperation.   (I. 2. 208–10)

When they reach the safety of the island, they seem to recover partly, but then Prospero deliberately contrives, through Ariel, a display of apparitions which drives the three most guilty into a more lasting fit of madness. At the end of Act three Alonso, Anthonio and Sebastian rush off in distraction. Interestingly, Gonzalo interprets their insanity not just as a reaction to the apparitions, but as a consequence of their own guilt:

> All three of them are desperate. Their great guilt,
> Like poison given to work a great time after,
> Now 'gins to bite the spirits.   (III. 3. 104–6)

It becomes clear that the suffering which Prospero had originally planned as a punishment for those who had injured him is also capable of acting as a cure. In Alonso's case particularly, the apparent loss of his son causes an

---

cerned with *The Tempest*. The most interesting allegorical reading is that of Colin Still, in *The Timeless Theme* (1936), which sees the whole play as an allegorical representation of ancient initiation ceremonies. We do not find such theories helpful, and deliberately omit any detailed consideration of them.

emotional crisis so fundamental as to produce a total change of personality. We do not have to turn to Elizabethan beliefs to explain this. Modern psychology too shows how shock treatment can be of use in the processes of brain-washing and indoctrination (see for example William Sargant's book *Battle for the Mind*). In the final scene this therapeutic madness is gradually cured, with the help of soothing music. Natural imagery of dawn breaking and the tide rising is beautifully used to convey the slow process by which they come to recognise Prospero, and themselves. Alonso resigns the usurped dukedom, and Gonzalo acknowledges the curative effect of their strange experiences: 'all of us [found] ourselves/ When no man was his own' (V. 1. 212–13). Thus the conversions of wicked men to goodness, which in *As You Like It* were merely conventional and took place off-stage, are here carried out before our eyes, in a way which we can recognise as representing the realities of life.

One goal of the play is the conversion and forgiveness of the wicked. Another is the fulfilment of young love, by which the younger generation can heal the enmities of the old. Here too, in the way he brings Ferdinand and Miranda together, Prospero acts as a psychiatrist, making them suffer in order that they shall value each other's love the more:

> this swift business
> I must uneasy make, lest too light winning
> Make the prize light. (I. 2. 453–5)

It may be that we shall find this psychological process less convincing than the punishment and cure of the wicked, partly because Ferdinand is already – to modern eyes, at least – an all too exquisitely virtuous young man. He does and says everything that is proper, and is little more than a symbol of princely virtue – the nearest approach to an allegorical figure that the play possesses. Moreover, in our time the premarital chastity on which Prospero insists

– with Ferdinand's full agreement – is apparently losing the high symbolic value it possessed for Shakespeare. But in any case the love story in *The Tempest* is subordinate to the moral and political theme: the disclosure of Ferdinand and Miranda playing chess in the final scene is one of the means Prospero uses to convert Alonso. Prospero conducts an elaborate psychiatric experiment, and it succeeds. We can recognise in him not just a fairytale enchanter but the 'magician' of our own days, the scientist, whether physicist or psychiatrist.

But Prospero is also a man like ourselves. He is not a conventional fairy godfather, mentioned only when required by the plot, and he differs from the scientist in having a deep emotional involvement in the subject-matter of his experiment. It is one of the great triumphs of *The Tempest* that we are allowed to enter into the experience of Prospero even more fully than into that of his victims or patients. He is, indeed, at the very centre of the play. In Act one, scene 2, he is pathetically anxious that Miranda should grasp his long-delayed explanation of how they came to be on the island, and we constantly feel his almost painful affection for her. This accounts for his harshness to Ferdinand: he may even feel a father's jealousy of his daughter's lover. It also accounts for the testiness with which he insists on their chastity: she is his 'loved darling' (III. 3. 93), and the severity towards Ferdinand is only the opposite side of his tenderness for her. There is some internal conflict, then, involved in Prospero's plan for his daughter's happiness. Still more is this the case with his plan for regaining his dukedom. After twelve years of waiting the chance has at last come for him to gain his revenge; it is essential that all should go well on this particular occasion, or, presumably, he will never achieve his aims; and so he is understandably nervous and ill-tempered. Hence the seeming cruelty of his reaction to Ariel's demand for liberty in Act one, scene 2, and the 'passion' he shows in Act four, scene 1, when he remembers the conspiracy of Caliban, Stephano and Trinculo. Above all, there is the conflict involved in his forgiveness of his enemies, a conflict that he himself describes as being between his 'fury' and his 'nobler reason' (V. 1. 26). Even after being touched by Ariel's sympathy, though he can forgive the repentant Alonso fairly readily, it is only with the greatest difficulty that he brings himself to pardon Anthonio – his own brother, who shows little sign of genuine repentance. 'I do forgive thee' is by no means a predictable conclusion to the following speech:

> Flesh and blood,
> You, brother mine, that entertained ambition,
> Expelled remorse and nature, who, with Sebastian –
> Whose inward pinches therefore are most strong –
> Would here have killed your King; I do forgive thee,
> Unnatural though thou art.   (V. 1. 74–9)

The jerky rhythms and tortured syntax enact a violent inward struggle. So far as the intended crime against Alonso is concerned, Prospero promises no more than that '*at this time*/ I will tell no tales' (V. 1. 128–9); and his final treatment of the conspiracy against himself is (understandably) far from warm.

This will be a convenient place to say a word more about these two island conspiracies. We have already said something of the conspiracy against Alonso, as being a repetition of the earlier conspiracy of Alonso and Anthonio against Prospero. If it succeeded, the usurper would be usurped; if it were not for Prospero's intervention, the series of usurpations would seem likely to go on for ever. And in the setting of a desert island, where all the tangible attractions of power are quite lacking, the repetition seems to lay bare an evil inseparable from human nature. The relevance of this sub-plot to the main plot of the play is clear; but the Caliban sub-plot might more easily be dismissed as 'comic relief' from serious matters. To do this, though, would be to under-estimate the extent to which the play is one about themes, such as usurpation and forgiveness, as well as about persons. It is normal in Elizabethan plays for sub-plots to offer a comic version of the same theme as the main plot. As Jan Kott puts it:

> Shakespearian dramas are constructed not on the principle of unity of action, but on the principle of analogy, comprising a double, treble, or quadruple plot, which repeats the same basic theme; they are a system of mirrors, as it were, both concave and convex, which reflect, magnify and parody the same situation.

In *The Tempest*, the sub-plot involving Caliban, Stephano and Trinculo offers yet another reflection of the theme of conspiracy and usurpation. It is a distorting mirror, which gives back a comically grotesque image of the plots of Anthonio and Alonso against Prospero and of Anthonio and Sebastian against Alonso, yet which only brings out the ugliness of conspiracy in a different way.

We have then in *The Tempest* a fairytale with a serious meaning; one which touches on important issues of conspiracy and usurpation, repentance and forgiveness, art and nature; one which turns potential tragedy into ultimate comedy. Yet the happiness of the happy ending is not handed to us without reservations. At the end of the play all is harmonious for the moment, but the future, outside the play, when the characters will have left the enchanted island for everyday reality, may not be so very happy after all. Shakespeare does not let us forget that plays come to an end, and he makes us wonder what might happen next: he does not claim, as fairytales do, that 'they all lived happily ever after'. It is important that, as we have remarked, the imaginary time of the play is the same as the real time of its performance. When the play is over, the real world continues; and this is something of which the Epilogue too reminds us. Prospero has given up the magical powers which have enabled him to give the play the shape it has, and now, an actor deprived of his role, he confronts an audience deprived of their illusion. There is nothing in this Epilogue to encourage us to identify Prospero with Shakespeare the man, retiring from the stage, as some critics have done. But there is much to suggest that we might equate the art of the magician with the Shakespearean art of the play itself – an art which must finally be cast off as we turn back to the everyday world.[1] Does this mean that the play, for all its apparent seriousness, can be seen as offering no more than an escape from reality after all? This is not our view of Shakespeare's meaning. The Epilogue goes on to speak in openly religious terms of the working of divine mercy in the real world:

> And my ending is despair,
> Unless I be relieved by prayer,
> Which pierces so that it assaults
> Mercy itself, and frees all faults.   (Ep. 15–18)

The audience could hardly fail to connect this with the theme of forgiveness in the play and with the play's references to miracles and to 'Providence divine'. In the twentieth century we may need to remind ourselves that for Shakespeare and his contemporaries God's merciful providence was a real part of the workings of the world, not just an idea. Without thinking of Prospero as 'being' or even 'standing for' the Christian God – and this again is a view that some critics have taken[2] – we can certainly see the events of *The Tempest* as offering a parallel to the course of the world as Shakespeare's contemporaries saw it. Moreover, if we turn back to Prospero's great speech about the masque in Act four, we shall see that he suggests a different kind of parallel between play and reality. The masque proved insubstantial: it melted away to nothing

---

[1] See Brockbank's article, mentioned in note 1, page 3.
[2] E.g. Colin Still.

before reaching a definite conclusion. But in this respect it was all the more like life, because

> like the baseless fabric of this vision,
> The cloud-capped towers, the gorgeous palaces,
> The solemn temples, the great globe itself,
> Yea, all which it inherit, shall dissolve,
> And like this insubstantial pageant faded,
> Leave not a rack behind.   (IV. I. 151–6)

The cut-short masque is surely a natural image of the play which contains it, and which ends *before* the characters sail back to Italy. Plays and masques do not last for ever, but in this they are like life itself.

This edition was completed in 1968, and consequently does not take account of work on *The Tempest* published since then.

THE CHARACTERS

ALONSO, King of Naples
SEBASTIAN, his brother
ANTHONIO, the usurping Duke of Milan, brother of Prospero
FERDINAND, son of Alonso
GONZALO, an honest old Councillor
ADRIAN ⎫
FRANCISCO ⎭ courtiers
Other courtiers in the service of Alonso and Anthonio

TRINCULO, a jester ⎫
STEPHANO, a drunken butler ⎭ in the service of Alonso
Master of the royal ship
Boatswain
Mariners

PROSPERO, the true Duke of Milan, brother of Anthonio
MIRANDA, his daughter
ARIEL, an airy spirit
CALIBAN, a savage and deformed slave

IRIS ⎫
CERES ⎪
JUNO ⎬ spirits in the masque
Nymphs ⎪
Reapers ⎭

Spirits in the shapes of dogs and hounds

ACT ONE, scene 1

*The scene is on board the royal ship, carrying King Alonso,
Duke Anthonio, and their party home from Tunis to Naples.
The play opens with dramatic abruptness, thrusting us into
the middle of the storm from which it takes its title.*

	Master *In charge of a ship under the direction of the Captain. He may perhaps have appeared on a balcony above, representing the poop, to speak to the Boatswain below.*
	Boatswain *Directs the sailors in carrying out the Master's orders.*
2	what cheer? *how are things going?*
3	Good *The naval way of acknowledging a subordinate's answer.*
3–4	fall to't yarely *get to work briskly*
4	run ourselves aground *The ship is evidently being blown too close to the island. The orders given next are intended to prevent this.*
6	Tend *Pay attention*
7	whistle *Both the Master and the Boatswain used a whistle to give their orders.*
7–8	Blow . . . enough! *Let the wind blow as much as it likes, so long as the ship can get enough room to manoeuvre*
10	Play the men *Act like men*
15	good *be* have the goodness to be
17	roarers *i.e. roaring waves; but the word also meant 'bullies', a sense drawn on here.*
22	Councillor *member of the King's Council*
22–24	if . . . more *if your authority as a Councillor extends to quelling the riot of the wind and waves, thus bringing about the peace there should be in the King's presence, there is no need for us sailors to do anything*
27	hap *happen*

28

ACT ONE

Scene 1. *A tempestuous noise of thunder and lightning heard. Enter* SHIP-MASTER *and* BOATSWAIN

MASTER   Boatswain!

BOATSWAIN Here, Master. What cheer?

MASTER   Good. Speak to the mariners: fall to't yarely, or we run ourselves aground. Bestir, bestir. [*Exit*

Enter MARINERS

BOATSWAIN Heigh, my hearts, cheerly, cheerly, my hearts. Yare, yare! Take in the topsail. Tend to the Master's whistle. Blow till thou burst thy wind, if room enough!

Enter ALONSO, SEBASTIAN, ANTHONIO, FERDINAND, GONZALO, *and* OTHERS

ALONSO   Good Boatswain, have care. Where's the Master? Play the men.   10

BOATSWAIN I pray now, keep below.

ANTHONIO Where is the Master, Boatswain?

BOATSWAIN Do you not hear him? You mar our labour; keep your cabins; you do assist the storm.

GONZALO   Nay, good be patient.

BOATSWAIN When the sea is. Hence, what cares these roarers for the name of King? To cabin – silence! Trouble us not.

GONZALO   Good, yet remember whom thou hast aboard.   20

BOATSWAIN   None that I love more than myself. You are a Councillor; if you can command these elements to silence and work the peace of the presence, we will not hand a rope more. Use your authority: if you cannot, give thanks you have lived so long, and make yourself ready in your cabin for the mischance of the hour, if it so hap. Cheerly, good hearts! Out of our way, I say. [*Exit*

30–1	his complexion ... gallows *his appearance suggests that he is sure to meet his death by hanging, not drowning*
31–2	Stand ... hanging *Let Fate keep the promise, apparently expressed in his villainous appearance, that he will be hanged*
32–3	make ... cable *may the hangman's rope to which he is destined act as our anchor-cable*
33	doth little advantage *is of little use to us*
35	Down ... topmast *Lowering the topmast was a way of stabilising a ship in a storm.*
36	Bring ... course *Take down all sails except the mainsail (a manoeuvre intended to keep the ship close to the wind and away from the shore).*
37–8	they ... office *the passengers are making more noise than the storm or than we do as we carry out our work*
39	give o'er *give up*
41–2	blasphemous *No blasphemies are given to the Boatswain in the text, but the actor may have been expected to 'ad lib' them.*
44	whoreson *(literally) son-of-a-whore*
47	I'll ... drowning *I'll guarantee that he won't be drowned*
49	unstanched wench *menstruating girl*
50	Lay her a-hold *Bring the ship close to the wind*
50–1	Set ... courses *put up the foresail in addition to the mainsail*
51	off ... off *head the ship out to sea (this should have been the result of laying the ship a-hold, if the storm had not been too powerful).*
53	must ... cold? *must we die without having a drink?*
54	assist *join*
56	merely *completely*

30

GONZALO   I have great comfort from this fellow.
   Methinks he hath no drowning mark upon him, his   30
   complexion is perfect gallows. Stand fast, good Fate,
   to his hanging; make the rope of his destiny our
   cable, for our own doth little advantage; if he be not
   born to be hanged, our case is miserable.
*They all go out. The stage is empty for a moment; the
       storm increases in force. Enter* BOATSWAIN
BOATSWAIN Down with the topmast! Yare, lower,
   lower! Bring her to try with main course.
                   A cry off stage
A plague upon this howling; they are louder than the
weather, or our office.

            Enter SEBASTIAN, ANTHONIO *and* GONZALO

Yet again? What do you here? Shall we give o'er and
drown, have you a mind to sink?   40
SEBASTIAN   A pox o' your throat, you bawling, blas-
phemous, incharitable dog!
BOATSWAIN Work you then.
ANTHONIO Hang, cur, hang, you whoreson, insolent
   noisemaker: we are less afraid to be drowned than
   thou art.
GONZALO   I'll warrant him for drowning, though the
   ship were no stronger than a nutshell, and as leaky
   as an unstanched wench.
BOATSWAIN Lay her a-hold, a-hold! Set her two   50
   courses: off to sea again, lay her off.

                Enter MARINERS, *wet*

MARINERS   All lost, to prayers, to prayers, all lost!
BOATSWAIN What, must our mouths be cold?
GONZALO   The King and Prince, at prayers – let's
                assist them,
        For our case is as theirs.
SEBASTIAN   I'm out of patience.
ANTHONIO We are merely cheated of our lives by
                drunkards.

                                                  31

57	wide-chopped *big-mouthed*
57–8	lie . . . tides *i.e. be punished even more severely than pirates, who were hanged on the sea-shore and left there until three tides had passed over them*
60	gape . . . him *open its mouth as wide as possible to swallow him up*
65–6	long . . . furze *Three shrubs that grow on dry ground.*
66	The wills above *The will of those above (i.e. the gods, or God)*
67	fain *willingly*

ACT ONE, scene 2

The quietness and leisure of this scene contrast strikingly with the noise and bustle of the one before. After briefly hurrying us into the midst of the action, Shakespeare now draws back and embarks on an elaborately artful explanation of all that led up to the storm. The scene is on Prospero's island, with perhaps some structure on the stage (or the inner stage, if there was one) representing his cell.

1	Art *i.e. magic*
4	welkin's cheek *sky's face*
6	brave *fine*
11	or ere *before*
13	fraughting *forming the ship's cargo*
14	amazement *terror*

This wide-chopped rascal – would thou
    mightst lie drowning
The washing of ten tides!

GONZALO   He'll be hanged yet,
Though every drop of water swear against it,
And gape at wid'st to glut him.

VOICES [*Shouting confusedly from off stage*] Mercy on us!   60
We split, we split! Farewell, my wife and children!
Farewell, brother! We split, we split, we split!

ANTHONIO Let's all sink with the King.

SEBASTIAN   Let's take leave of him.
            [*Exeunt* ANTHONIO *and* SEBASTIAN

GONZALO   Now would I give a thousand furlongs of
sea for an acre of barren ground: long heath, broom,
furze, anything. The wills above be done, but I would
fain die a dry death.   [*Exeunt*

Scene 2. *Enter* PROSPERO *and* MIRANDA

MIRANDA If by your Art, my dearest father, you have
Put the wild waters in this roar, allay them.
The sky it seems would pour down stinking
    pitch,
But that the sea, mounting to the welkin's
    cheek,
Dashes the fire out. O, I have suffered
With those that I saw suffer: a brave vessel,
Who had no doubt some noble creature in her,
Dashed all to pieces! O, the cry did knock
Against my very heart. Poor souls, they perished.
Had I been any god of power, I would   10
Have sunk the sea within the earth, or ere
It should the good ship so have swallowed, and
The fraughting souls within her.

PROSPERO   Be collected;
No more amazement. Tell your piteous heart
There's no harm done.

19	more better *of higher rank*
20	cell *small, solitary dwelling*
21	no greater *i.e. than the man he has just described himself as being*
22	meddle *mingle*

25	Art *i.e. the magic garment, which confers magical powers on its wearer, and thus symbolises Prospero's art of magic. Perhaps as he lays it down the noises of thunder representing the storm might die away.*
26	direful *dreadful*
	wrack *wreck*
27	virtue *essence*
28	provision *foresight*
29	soul *i.e. soul lost. In Shakespeare's later plays, ideas and images come so fast that it often happens that a speaker will begin on a second construction before completing the first.*
30	perdition *loss. The word was commonly used in a theological sense to mean 'damnation', and may therefore have been suggested by 'soul' in the previous line.*
31	Betid *Happened*
35	bootless inquisition *profitless questioning*

41	Out *Fully*

MIRANDA   O woe the day!
PROSPERO   No harm.
    I have done nothing but in care of thee,
    Of thee my dear one, thee my daughter, who
    Art ignorant of what thou art, nought knowing
    Of whence I am, nor that I am more better
    Than Prospero, master of a full poor cell,   20
    And thy no greater father.
MIRANDA   More to know
    Did never meddle with my thoughts.
PROSPERO   'Tis time
    I should inform thee farther. Lend thy hand
    And pluck my magic garment from me. So,
                Lays down his mantle
    Lie there my Art. Wipe thou thine eyes, have
        comfort.
    The direful spectacle of the wrack, which touched
    The very virtue of compassion in thee,
    I have with such provision in mine Art
    So safely ordered that there is no soul –
    No, not so much perdition as an hair,   30
    Betid to any creature in the vessel
    Which thou heard'st cry, which thou saw'st
        sink. Sit down,
    For thou must now know farther.
MIRANDA   You have often
    Begun to tell me what I am, but stopped
    And left me to a bootless inquisition,
    Concluding, 'Stay, not yet'.
PROSPERO   The hour's now come.
    The very minute bids thee ope thine ear,
    Obey, and be attentive. Canst thou remember
    A time before we came unto this cell?
    I do not think thou canst, for then thou wast not 40
    Out three years old.
MIRANDA   Certainly, sir, I can.
PROSPERO By what? by any other house, or person?

                                                    35

43–4	Of any thing . . . remembrance *Tell me about the picture of anything at all that you still have in your memory*
46–7	assurance . . . warrants *certainty that my memory guarantees*
48	tended *attended*
50	backward . . . time *abyss of time past*
51–2	If thou . . . mayst *If you can remember anything of the time before you came to this island, you may remember how you came to it*
54	Milan *Throughout the play this word should be stressed on the first syllable (as 'millan' in 'Macmillan').*
56	piece of virtue *perfect example of chastity*
59	no worse issued *of no lower birth*
63	holp *helped*
64	teen . . . you to *trouble I have caused you*
65	from *out of*
66	My brother . . . *The speech beginning here is twisted and almost shattered by the pain and anger it causes Prospero to recollect these shameful events – hence the difficulty we sometimes have in following it. He is absorbed in his vivid memories, and at times is almost thinking aloud, yet he is also pitifully anxious that Miranda should listen and understand, and keeps on demanding reassurance that she is attending.*

36

Of any thing the image, tell me, that
Hath kept with thy remembrance.

MIRANDA   'Tis far off,
And rather like a dream than an assurance
That my remembrance warrants: had I not
Four or five women once, that tended me?

PROSPERO Thou hadst, and more, Miranda. But how is
it
That this lives in thy mind? What seest thou
else
In the dark backward and abysm of time?   50
If thou remember'st aught ere thou cam'st here,
How thou cam'st here thou mayst.

MIRANDA   But that I do not.

PROSPERO Twelve year since, Miranda, twelve year
since,
Thy father was the Duke of Milan and
A prince of power.

MIRANDA   Sir, are not you my father?

PROSPERO Thy mother was a piece of virtue, and
She said thou wast my daughter; and thy father
Was Duke of Milan, and his only heir
A Princess, no worse issued.

MIRANDA   O the heavens,
What foul play had we, that we came from
thence?   60
Or blessèd was't we did?

PROSPERO   Both, both, my girl.
By foul play, as thou say'st, were we heaved
thence,
But blessedly holp hither.

MIRANDA   O my heart bleeds
To think o' the teen that I have turned you to,
Which is from my remembrance. Please you,
farther.

PROSPERO My brother and thy uncle, called Anthonio –
I pray thee mark me, that a brother should

68–9	next . . . loved *I loved best in the world, after yourself*
69–70	put . . . state *gave the management of my dukedom*
71	Through . . . signories *Among all the Italian states*
72	prime *leading*
73	liberal arts *Roughly what we would now call 'culture'.*
74	those *i.e. the liberal arts*
76–7	to my . . . rapt in *withdrew from my responsibilities as Duke, being completely carried away by*
79–87	Being . . . out on't *Having once acquired a perfect knowledge of how to grant or refuse requests, and of which men to promote, which to keep in check for their excessive ambition, he completely changed those who owed their advancement to me, either by putting others in their place, or by so influencing my supporters as to turn them against me. Thus, gaining control over both the officials and their departments, he was able to do what he liked with the people in general. In this way, he treated me as the ivy does a tree which supports it – first uses it to raise itself, then sucks up its vitality*
83	key *The 'keys of office' suggest musical keys, and hence* tune
88	mark me *attend to what I say*
90	closeness *privacy*
91–2	that which . . . rate *those studies which, if only by being so private, went beyond the common people's power to value them*
94	parent *The idea here is that expressed by Miranda a little later, when she says 'Good wombs have borne bad sons'. Prospero's trustfulness encouraged his brother's disloyalty.*
	did beget . . . was *produced in him a disloyalty opposite to, and as great as, my trust*
97	sans bound *without limit*
97–105	He being . . . prerogative *Having thus gained possession both of my normal income and of such additions as could be demanded in my name, he then – like someone who, by telling the same lie again and again, had made his memory such a sinner against truth that he believed his own lie – came to believe that he really was the Duke, as a result of playing my part, and enjoying all my power, honour and privileges*

38

Be so perfidious – he, whom next thyself
Of all the world I loved, and to him put
The manage of my state, as at that time   70
Through all the signories it was the first,
And Prospero the prime duke, being so reputed
In dignity, and for the liberal arts
Without a parallel; those being all my study,
The government I cast upon my brother,
And to my state grew stranger, being transported
And rapt in secret studies. Thy false uncle –
Dost thou attend me?

MIRANDA   Sir, most heedfully.

PROSPERO Being once pèrfected how to grant suits,
How to deny them, who t'advance, and who   80
To trash for over-topping, new created
The creatures that were mine, I say, or changed
    'em,
Or else new formed 'em; having both the key
Of officer and office, set all hearts i' the state
To what tune pleased his ear, that now he was
The ivy which had hid my princely trunk,
And sucked my verdure out on't. Thou attend'st
    not?

MIRANDA O good sir, I do.

PROSPERO   I pray thee mark me.
I thus neglecting worldly ends, all dedicated
To closeness and the bettering of my mind   90
With that which, but by being so retired,
O'er-prized all popular rate, in my false brother
Awaked an evil nature; and my trust,
Like a good parent, did beget of him
A falsehood in its contrary as great
As my trust was, which had indeed no limit,
A confidence sans bound. He being thus lorded,
Not only with what my revènue yielded,
But what my power might else exact, like one
Who having into truth, by telling of it,   100

Made such a sinner of his memory
To credit his own lie, he did believe
He was indeed the Duke, out o' the substitution
And executing th'outward face of royalty
With all prerogative. Hence his ambition
   growing –
Dost thou hear?

MIRANDA   Your tale, sir, would cure deafness.

PROSPERO To have no screen between this part he
   played
And him he played it for, he needs will be
Absolute Milan. Me, poor man, my library
Was dukedom large enough. Of temporal
   royalties   110
He thinks me now incapable, confederates,
So dry he was for sway, wi' the King of Naples
To give him annual tribute, do him homage,
Subject his coronet to his crown and bend
The Dukedom yet unbowed – alas, poor Milan! –
To most ignoble stooping.

MIRANDA   O the heavens!

PROSPERO Mark his condition and th'event, then tell me
If this might be a brother.

MIRANDA   I should sin
To think but nobly of my grandmother;
Good wombs have borne bad sons.

PROSPERO   Now the condition. 120
This King of Naples, being an enemy
To me inveterate, hearkens my brother's suit,
Which was that he, in lieu o' the premises
Of homage, and I know not how much tribute,
Should presently extìrpate me and mine
Out of the Dukedom, and confer fair Milan
With all the honours on my brother. Whereon,
A treacherous army levied, one midnight
Fated to the purpose, did Anthonio open
The gates of Milan, and i' the dead of darkness 130

131 ministers . . . purpose *those employed in this matter*

134-5 hint . . . to 't *occasion that forces tears from my eyes*

138 impertinent *irrelevant*

141-2 nor . . . business *nor did they want to make the affair appear so murderous*

144 In few *To put it briefly*
bark *vessel*

146 butt *tub (i.e. poor, unseaworthy boat)*

150-1 whose . . . wrong *Prospero supposes that the winds 'sighed' (i.e. blew) out of pity for the castaways, and thus accidentally made their plight worse even while showing sympathy for them.*

155 decked *covered*

156-8 raised . . . ensue *gave me the spirit to endure courageously whatever might happen*

The ministers for the purpose hurried thence
Me, and thy crying self.

MIRANDA   Alack, for pity!
I, not remembering how I cried out then,
Will cry it o'er again. It is a hint
That wrings mine eyes to 't.

PROSPERO   Hear a little further,
And then I'll bring thee to the present business
Which now's upon's, without the which this
     story
Were most impertinent.

MIRANDA   Wherefore did they not
That hour destroy us?

PROSPERO   Well demanded, wench:
My tale provokes that question. Dear, they
     durst not,   140
So dear the love my people bore me; nor set
A mark so bloody on the business; but
With colours fairer painted their foul ends.
In few, they hurried us aboard a bark,
Bore us some leagues to sea, where they prepared
A rotten carcass of a butt, not rigged,
Nor tackle, sail nor mast – the very rats
Instinctively have quit it. There they hoist us,
To cry to the sea, that roared to us; to sigh
To the winds, whose pity sighing back again   150
Did us but loving wrong.

MIRANDA   Alack, what trouble
Was I then to you?

PROSPERO   O, a cherubin
Thou wast that did preserve me. Thou didst
     smile,
Infusèd with a fortitude from heaven,
When I have decked the sea with drops full salt,
Under my burden groaned; which raised in me
An undergoing stomach, to bear up
Against what should ensue.

43

162   who being then *he having been*

165   steaded much *been very useful*
        gentleness *noble generosity*
166   furnished *provided*

168–9   Would . . . man! *If only I could see that man one day!*

172–3   made . . . can *made you benefit more by your education
                than other royal children*

179   Now my dear Lady *Who is now my generous benefactress*

181   zenith *highest point of my fortunes*
182   star *According to astrology, which was widely believed in
                in Shakespeare's time, the heavenly bodies could
                exercise a determining power (or 'influence') over
                men's lives. If Prospero does not take advantage of
                their present favourable position, he will always be
                dogged by ill fortune.*
183   omit *neglect*
185   dulness *drowsiness*

44

MIRANDA   How came we ashore?

PROSPERO By Providence divine.
          Some food we had, and some fresh water, that   160
          A noble Neapolitan, Gonzalo,
          Out of his charity – who being then appointed
          Master of this design – did give us, with
          Rich garments, linens, stuffs and necessaries
          Which since have steaded much; so, of his
               gentleness,
          Knowing I loved my books, he furnished me
          From mine own library with volumes that
          I prize above my Dukedom.

MIRANDA   Would I might
          But ever see that man!

PROSPERO   Now I arise,
          Sit still, and hear the last of our sea-sorrow.   170
          Here in this island we arrived, and here
          Have I, thy schoolmaster, made thee more profit
          Than other princes can, that have more time
          For vainer hours, and tutors not so careful.

MIRANDA Heaven thank you for't. And now I pray you,
               sir,
          For still 'tis beating in my mind, your reason
          For raising this sea-storm?

PROSPERO   Know thus far forth:
          By accident most strange, bountiful Fortune
          (Now my dear Lady) hath mine enemies
          Brought to this shore; and by my prescience   180
          I find my zenith doth depend upon
          A most auspicious star, whose influence
          If now I court not, but omit, my fortunes
          Will ever after droop. Here cease more questions,
          Thou art inclined to sleep; 'tis a good dulness,
          And give it way; I know thou canst not choose.

                    MIRANDA *falls asleep*
          Come away, servant, come. I am ready now,
          Approach my Ariel. Come.   [*Enter* ARIEL

192   to thy . . . task *test with your most difficult commands*
             ('task' here being a verb)

193   quality *subordinate spirits*

194   Performed to point *Produced exactly*

195   article *detail*

196   beak *prow*

197   waist *amidships*
             deck *poop*

198   flamed amazement *caused terror by appearing as flames.
             Ariel was appearing in the form of St Elmo's fire.*

200   boresprit *bowsprit*
             distinctly *in several places*

203   sight-outrunning *moving faster than the eye could
             follow*

204   Neptune *The god of the sea, who was represented as
             carrying a 'trident' (three-pronged sceptre) as his
             emblem.*

207   coil *uproar*

208   infect *affect*

213   up-staring *standing on end*

ARIEL All hail, great master, grave sir, hail! I come
    To answer thy best pleasure; be't to fly,   190
    To swim, to dive into the fire, to ride
    On the curled clouds; to thy strong bidding task
    Ariel and all his quality.

PROSPERO   Hast thou, spirit,
    Performed to point the tempest that I bade
    thee?

ARIEL To every article.
    I boarded the King's ship; now on the beak,
    Now in the waist, the deck, in every cabin,
    I flamed amazement; sometime I'd divide
    And burn in many places; on the topmast,
    The yards and boresprit would I flame distinctly, 200
    Then meet, and join. Jove's lightning, the
        precursors
    O' the dreadful thunder-claps, more momentary
    And sight-outrunning were not; the fire and
        cracks
    Of sulphurous roaring the most mighty Neptune
    Seem to besiege, and make his bold waves
        tremble,
    Yea, his dread trident shake.

PROSPERO   My brave spirit,
    Who was so firm, so constant, that this coil
    Would not infect his reason?

ARIEL   Not a soul
    But felt a fever of the mad, and played
    Some tricks of desperation; all but mariners   210
    Plunged in the foaming brine, and quit the
        vessel,
    Then all afire with me. The King's son
        Ferdinand,
    With hair up-staring then, like reeds, not hair,
    Was the first man that leaped; cried, 'Hell is
        empty,
    And all the devils are here.'

PROSPERO   Why, that's my spirit!
          But was not this nigh shore?
ARIEL   Close by, my master.
PROSPERO But are they, Ariel, safe?
ARIEL   Not a hair perished:
          On their sustaining garments not a blemish,
          But fresher than before; and, as thou bad'st me,
          In troops I have dispersed them 'bout the isle. 220
          The King's son have I landed by himself,
          Whom I left cooling of the air with sighs,
          In an odd angle of the isle, and sitting,
          His arms in this sad knot.
PROSPERO   Of the King's ship,
          The mariners, say how thou hast disposed,
          And all the rest o' the fleet.
ARIEL   Safely in harbour
          Is the King's ship, in the deep nook where once
          Thou call'dst me up at midnight to fetch dew
          From the still-vexed Bermoothes – there she's
              hid;
          The mariners all under hatches stowed,   230
          Who, with a charm joined to their suffered
              labour,
          I have left asleep. And, for the rest o' the fleet,
          Which I dispersed, they all have met again
          And are upon the Mediterranean flote
          Bound sadly home for Naples,
          Supposing that they saw the King's ship
              wracked
          And his great person perish.
PROSPERO   Ariel, thy charge
          Exactly is performed; but there's more work.
          What is the time o' the day?
ARIEL   Past the mid season.
PROSPERO At least two glasses. The time 'twixt six and
              now   240
          Must by us both be spent most preciously.

49

242   pains *labours*

243   remember thee *remind you of*

244   **How now?** . . . *The anger with which Prospero meets Ariel's reminder may seem cruel; but the role of Prospero should not be sentimentalised. He is capable of great sternness as well as great affection, and, in the world of this play, where evil is so powerful, good cannot afford to be too mild. This is a lesson that Prospero himself has learned by bitter experience. In this particular case, it is desperately important, as he has just been explaining to Miranda, that he should make use of a uniquely favourable conjunction of heavenly influences, and so Ariel has been tactless in his choice of moment to request his freedom. Moreover, for Shakespeare, Prospero's anger gives an excuse for us to be told something of the background of Ariel and Caliban.*

250   bate me *let me off*

255   veins *It was supposed that water ran beneath the earth like blood in the human veins.*

256   baked *hardened*

258   envy *malice*

259   grown . . . hoop *bent double*

262   Argier *Algiers*

           was she so? *she was, was she?*

265   mischiefs *wicked deeds*

ARIEL Is there more toil? Since thou dost give me pains,
  Let me remember thee what thou hast promised
  Which is not yet performed me.
PROSPERO   How now? moody?
  What is't thou canst demand?
ARIEL   My liberty.
PROSPERO Before the time be out? No more!
ARIEL   I prithee,
  Remember I have done thee worthy service,
  Told thee no lies, made no mistakings, served
  Without or grudge or grumblings; thou didst
   promise
  To bate me a full year.
PROSPERO   Dost thou forget   250
  From what a torment I did free thee?
ARIEL   No.
PROSPERO Thou dost; and think'st it much to tread the
   ooze
  Of the salt deep,
  To run upon the sharp wind of the north,
  To do me business in the veins o' th' earth
  When it is baked with frost.
ARIEL   I do not, sir.
PROSPERO Thou liest, malignant thing. Hast thou forgot
  The foul witch Sycorax, who with age and
   envy
  Was grown into a hoop? Hast thou forgot her?
ARIEL No, sir.   260
PROSPERO Thou hast: where was she born? Speak;
   tell me.
ARIEL Sir, in Argier.
PROSPERO   O, was she so? I must
  Once in a month recount what thou hast been,
  Which thou forget'st. This damned witch
   Sycorax,
  For mischiefs manifold and sorceries terrible
  To enter human hearing, from Argier

267   one . . . did *Her condition may have saved her life: pregnant women were not put to death.*

270   blue-eyed *with blue eyelids (a supposed sign of pregnancy)*

273   for *because*

274   earthy *Sycorax is a creature of the earth, and her son, Caliban, follows her in this; but Ariel is 'an airy spirit', and what was 'earthy' would therefore be abhorrent to him.*

275   grand hests *great commands*

276   more . . . ministers *spirits in her service more powerful than yourself*

277   unmitigable *unappeasable; incapable of being calmed*

281   vent *express*

282   strike *strike the water*

296   his *its*

	Thou know'st was banished – for one thing she did	
	They would not take her life. Is not this true?	
ARIEL	Ay, sir.	
PROSPERO	This blue-eyed hag was hither brought with child,	270

PROSPERO This blue-eyed hag was hither brought with
  child,   270
  And here was left by the sailors. Thou, my slave,
  As thou report'st thyself, was then her servant;
  And, for thou wast a spirit too delicate
  To act her earthy and abhorred commands,
  Refusing her grand hests, she did confine thee
  By help of her more potent ministers,
  And in her most unmitigable rage,
  Into a cloven pine, within which rift
  Imprisoned, thou didst painfully remain
  A dozen years; within which space she died, 280
  And left thee there, where thou didst vent thy
    groans
  As fast as mill-wheels strike. Then was this
    island
  (Save for the son that she did litter here,
  A freckled whelp, hag-born) not honoured with
  A human shape.

ARIEL   Yes: Caliban her son.

PROSPERO Dull thing, I say so – he, that Caliban
  Whom now I keep in service. Thou best know'st
  What torment I did find thee in; thy groans
  Did make wolves howl, and penetrate the breasts
  Of ever-angry bears; it was a torment 290
  To lay upon the damned, which Sycorax
  Could not again undo. It was mine Art,
  When I arrived, and heard thee, that made gape
  The pine, and let thee out.

ARIEL   I thank thee, master.

PROSPERO If thou more murmur'st, I will rend an oak
  And peg thee in his knotty entrails till
  Thou hast howled away twelve winters.

298   correspondent *obedient*

299   do . . . gently *perform my services as a spirit graciously*

302   subject *visible. The invisibility of a magician or spirit
was an accepted convention of the Elizabethan stage,
and a special cloak to indicate invisibility was sometimes worn.*

308   Heaviness *Sleepiness*

312   miss *do without*

313–14   serves . . . us *performs duties that are useful to us*

Off-stage *There may have been a semi-permanent structure on the stage to represent Caliban's den, in which
case Caliban would perhaps be hiding behind it and
not completely off the stage.*

318   When? *When are you coming?*

319   quaint *ingenious*

54

ARIEL   Pardon, master;
    I will be correspondent to command
    And do my spriting gently.
PROSPERO   Do so; and after two days
    I will discharge thee.
ARIEL   That's my noble master!   300
    What shall I do? say what? what shall I do?
PROSPERO Go make thyself like a nymph o' the sea, be
        subject to
    No sight but thine and mine: invisible
    To every eyeball else. Go take this shape
    And hither come in't; go: hence with diligence.
                                    [*Exit* ARIEL
    [To MIRANDA] Awake, dear heart, awake, thou
        hast slept well.
    Awake.
MIRANDA   The strangeness of your story put
    Heaviness in me.
PROSPERO   Shake it off. Come on,
    We'll visit Caliban, my slave, who never
    Yields us kind answer.
MIRANDA   'Tis a villain, sir,   310
    I do not love to look on.
PROSPERO   But, as 'tis,
    We cannot miss him: he does make our fire,
    Fetch in our wood, and serves in offices
    That profit us. What ho! slave! Caliban!
    Thou earth, thou! speak.
CALIBAN [*Off-stage*]   There's wood enough within.
PROSPERO Come forth, I say, there's other business for
        thee.
    Come, thou tortoise. When?
            Enter ARIEL *like a water-nymph*
    Fine apparition! My quaint Ariel,
    Hark in thine ear.   [*Whispers to* ARIEL
ARIEL   My lord, it shall be done.
                                            [*Exit*

320   got *begotten*

321   dam *mother*

322   wicked *poisonous. For all his 'earthy' and evil qualities, Caliban's language can be breathtakingly beautiful, as it is in this curse.*

327   urchins *goblins*

328   for . . . work *throughout the desolation of the night, when evil spirits are permitted to be active*

329   exercise *set to work*

330   As thick as honeycomb *With pinches as close together as the cells of a honeycomb*

331   'em *the cells*

332   by *by inheritance from*

PROSPERO Thou poisonous slave, got by the devil himself   320
          Upon thy wicked dam, come forth.

                         Enter CALIBAN

CALIBAN As wicked dew as e'er my mother brushed
          With raven's feather from unwholesome fen
          Drop on you both; a South-west blow on ye,
          And blister you all o'er.

PROSPERO For this, be sure tonight thou shalt have cramps,
          Side-stitches that shall pen thy breath up; urchins
          Shall, for that vast of night that they may work,
          All exercise on thee; thou shalt be pinched
          As thick as honeycomb, each pinch more stinging   330
          Than bees that made 'em.

CALIBAN   I must eat my dinner.
          This island's mine by Sycorax my mother,
          Which thou tak'st from me. When thou camest first
          Thou strok'dst me, and made much of me; wouldst give me
          Water with berries in't, and teach me how
          To name the bigger light and how the less,
          That burn by day and night; and then I loved thee,
          And showed thee all the qualities o' th' isle,
          The fresh springs, brine-pits, barren place and fertile –
          Cursed be I that I did so. All the charms   340
          Of Sycorax, toads, beetles, bats, light on you;
          For I am all the subjects that you have,
          Which first was mine own king; and here you sty me
          In this hard rock, whiles you do keep from me
          The rest o' th' island.

57

346   stripes *lashes*

351   I . . . else *otherwise I would have populated*

352–63   Abhorrèd . . . prison *Though this speech is given to Miranda in the Folio, many editors have felt that the forcefulness of its anger is better suited to Prospero, and have transferred it to him.*

353   print *impression. The image is of blank metal or wax being stamped with a design.*

354   capable . . . ill *able to be stamped with any evil*

358   endowed . . . With *gave your meanings*

359   thy vile race *the ignoble nature you have inherited*

365   rid *destroy. Plague, among the symptoms of which were red spots, was common in Shakespeare's England.*

366   Hag-seed *Offspring of a hag*

367   thou'rt best *you had better*

370   old cramps *the cramps of old age*

371   aches *Pronounced 'aitches'.*

PROSPERO   Thou most lying slave,
          Whom stripes may move, not kindness! I have
              used thee –
          Filth as thou art – with humane care, and
              lodged thee
          In mine own cell, till thou didst seek to violate
          The honour of my child.
CALIBAN Oh ho, oh ho, would't had been done!   350
          Thou didst prevent me, I had peopled else
          This isle with Calibans.
MIRANDA   Abhorrèd slave,
          Which any print of goodness wilt not take,
          Being capable of all ill! I pitied thee,
          Took pains to make thee speak, taught thee
              each hour
          One thing or other. When thou didst not, savage,
          Know thine own meaning, but wouldst gabble,
              like
          A thing most brutish, I endowed thy purposes
          With words that made them known; but thy vile
              race,
          Though thou didst learn, had that in't which
              good natures   360
          Could not abide to be with; therefore wast thou
          Deservedly confined into this rock,
          Who hadst deserved more than a prison.
CALIBAN You taught me language, and my profit on't
          Is, I know how to curse. The red plague rid you
          For learning me your language!
PROSPERO   Hag-seed, hence!
          Fetch us in fuel, and be quick, thou'rt best,
          To answer other business. Shrug'st thou,
              malice?
          If thou neglect'st, or dost unwillingly
          What I command, I'll rack thee with old cramps, 370
          Fill all thy bones with aches, make thee roar,
          That beasts shall tremble at thy din.

                                                        59

375	vassal *slave*
379	whist *being silenced*
380	featly *nimbly*
382	burden *refrain. This is supplied by the animal noises off-stage.*
387	strain *tune*
	Chanticleer *The conventional name for a cock.*
390	waits *attends*
392	wrack *wreck*
398	Full . . . lies *Your father's body is drowned under a full five fathoms of water. (A fathom is six feet.)*
401-2	Nothing . . . suffer *There is no corruptible part of him that does not undergo*

CALIBAN   No, pray thee.
       [*Aside*] I must obey; his Art is of such power
       It would control my dam's god Setebos,
       And make a vassal of him.
PROSPERO   So, slave, hence. [*Exit* CALIBAN
Enter ARIEL, *invisible, playing and singing, followed by*
              FERDINAND. ARIEL *sings*
       Come unto these yellow sands,
           And then take hands.
       Curtsied when you have and kissed,
           The wild waves whist,
       Foot it featly here and there   380
       And sweet sprites bear
           The burden. Hark, hark!
VOICES [*Here and there off-stage*] Bow-wow!
ARIEL   The watch-dogs bark.
VOICES [*Off*] Bow-wow!
ARIEL   Hark, hark! I hear
       The strain of strutting Chanticleer
           cry –
VOICES [*Off*]   Cock-a-diddle-dow!
FERDINAND Where should this music be? I' th' air, or
           th'earth?
       It sounds no more; and sure it waits upon   390
       Some god o' th' island. Sitting on a bank,
       Weeping again the king my father's wrack,
       This music crept by me upon the waters,
       Allaying both their fury and my passion
       With its sweet air: thence have I followed it,
       Or it hath drawn me rather, but 'tis gone.
       No, it begins again.
                    ARIEL *sings*
       Full fathom five thy father lies;
           Of his bones are coral made;
       Those are pearls that were his eyes;   400
           Nothing of him that doth fade
       But doth suffer a sea-change

408   ditty does remember *words of the song commemorate*

410   That . . . owes *Belonging to the earth*
411   fringèd curtains *eyelids fringed with eyelashes*
      advance *lift up*
412   yond *over there*

414   carries . . . form *has a fine appearance*

417   but *except that*

418   that's . . . canker *which is what corrodes beauty*

421   natural *mortal*

422   It goes on *My plan works*

424–5 Most . . . attend! *As Ferdinand has remarked earlier, he*
      is sure that the mysterious music is attending a god.
425   Vouchsafe . . . remain *Grant my prayer that I may*
      know whether you dwell

428   bear me *behave myself*
      prime *major*

Into something rich and strange.
Sea-nymphs hourly ring his knell.

VOICES [*Off-stage*]   Ding-dong.

ARIEL   Hark now I hear them.

VOICES [*Off*]   Ding-dong bell.

FERDINAND The ditty does remember my drowned
          father.
     This is no mortal business, nor no sound
     That the earth owes. I hear it now above me.   410

PROSPERO [*To* MIRANDA] The fringèd curtains of thine
          eye advance,
     And say what thou seest yond.

MIRANDA   What is't? a spirit?
     Lord, how it looks about. Believe me, sir,
     It carries a brave form. But 'tis a spirit.

PROSPERO No, wench, it eats, and sleeps, and hath such
          senses
     As we have – such. This gallant which thou seest
     Was in the wrack, and, but he's something
          stained
     With grief (that's beauty's canker), thou mightst
          call him
     A goodly person. He hath lost his fellows,
     And strays about to find 'em.

MIRANDA   I might call him   420
     A thing divine, for nothing natural
     I ever saw so noble.

PROSPERO [*Aside*]   It goes on, I see,
     As my soul prompts it. Spirit, fine spirit, I'll
          free thee
     Within two days for this.

FERDINAND   Most sure the goddess
     On whom these airs attend! Vouchsafe my
          prayer
     May know if you remain upon this island,
     And that you will some good instruction give
     How I may bear me here. My prime request,

430   maid *Ferdinand probably means 'a girl' (not a goddess);
             Miranda in her answer perhaps uses the word to mean
             'virgin'.*

432   best *person of highest rank (because he is now King of
             Naples, his father being, as he supposes, dead).*

435–6   A single ... Naples *I would be what I am now, a solitary,
             helpless creature, astonished to hear you mention
             Naples*
436   He *i.e. the King of Naples. (A ruler was often known
             simply by the name of his state, as occurs in the next
             line.)*
438   never ... ebb *which have never stopped weeping since*

441   twain *two of them. We hear nothing more of this son of
             Anthonio's.*
442   more braver *even finer. There is possibly a pun on
             'brave' meaning courageous (as applied to Anthonio's
             son) and 'brave' meaning fine (as applied to Miranda).*
             control thee *prove you wrong*
444   changed eyes *fallen in love*
             Delicate *Skilful*

446   done ... wrong *made a slight mistake (ironically polite)*

449–50   Pity ... way *May compassion for me influence my
             father to consider my side of the matter*

451   your ... forth *if your affections are not already engaged*

Which I do last pronounce, is – O you wonder –
If you be maid, or no?

MIRANDA   No wonder, sir,   430
But certainly a maid.

FERDINAND   My language? Heavens!
I am the best of them that speak this speech,
Were I but where 'tis spoken.

PROSPERO   How? the best?
What wert thou if the King of Naples heard
      thee?

FERDINAND A single thing, as I am now, that wonders
To hear thee speak of Naples. He does hear me,
And that he does, I weep. Myself am Naples,
Who with mine eyes, never since at ebb, beheld
The King my father wracked.

MIRANDA   Alack, for mercy.

FERDINAND Yes, faith, and all his lords, the Duke of
      Milan   440
And his brave son being twain.

PROSPERO [*Aside*]   The Duke of Milan
And his more braver daughter could control
      thee
If now 'twere fit to do't. At the first sight
They have changed eyes. Delicate Ariel,
I'll set thee free for this. [*To* FERDINAND] A word,
      good sir,
I fear you have done yourself some wrong; a
      word.

MIRANDA [*Aside*] Why speaks my father so ungently?
      This
Is the third man that e'er I saw, the first
That e'er I sighed for. Pity move my father
To be inclined my way!

FERDINAND   O, if a virgin,   450
And your affection not gone forth, I'll make you
The Queen of Naples.

PROSPERO   Soft, sir, one word more.

453   either's *the other's*

454   uneasy *difficult*

454–5   lest . . . prize light *in case winning each other's love too easily should make them value it insufficiently. There is a pun on two senses of 'light', as 'easy' and 'unimportant'.*

457   name *i.e. King of Naples*
ow'st *possessest*

460   temple *Ferdinand's body. Miranda is arguing that no evil soul could inhabit such an attractive body; she goes on to explain that if an evil spirit did live there, good spirits would want to live there too; which, she assumes, would be absurd.*

468   entertainment *treatment*

471   gentle . . . fearful *of noble birth and not cowardly*

472   My . . . tutor? *Shall an inferior offshoot of mine tell me what to do?*

474   from thy ward *leave your defensive stance*

475   stick *i.e. his magic wand*

66

[*Aside*] They are both in either's powers; but
  this swift business
I must uneasy make, lest too light winning
Make the prize light. [*To* FERDINAND] One word
  more. I charge thee
That thou attend me. Thou dost here usurp
The name thou ow'st not, and hast put thyself
Upon this island as a spy, to win it
From me, the lord on't.

FERDINAND   No, as I am a man.

MIRANDA There's nothing ill can dwell in such a temple; 460
If the ill spirit have so fair a house,
Good things will strive to dwell with't.

PROSPERO   Follow me.
[*To* MIRANDA] Speak not you for him; he's a
  traitor. [*To* FERDINAND] Come,
I'll manacle thy neck and feet together,
Sea-water shalt thou drink, thy food shall be
The fresh-brook mussels, withered roots, and
  husks
Wherein the acorn cradled. Follow.

FERDINAND   No,
I will resist such entertainment, till
Mine enemy has more power.
He draws his sword, but PROSPERO's *magic prevents
  him from moving*

MIRANDA   O dear father,
Make not too rash a trial of him, for   470
He's gentle, and not fearful.

PROSPERO   What, I say,
My foot my tutor? Put thy sword up, traitor,
Who mak'st a show, but dar'st not strike, thy
  conscience
Is so possessed with guilt. Come, from thy
  ward,
For I can here disarm thee with this stick,
And make thy weapon drop.

478 I'll . . . surety *I'll guarantee his good behaviour*

483 To the most *Compared to the majority*

487 *nerves* sinews

491 nor . . . threats *and even the threats of this man*

494-5 all . . . use of *those who are free are welcome to every other part of the world*

MIRANDA   Beseech you, father.
PROSPERO Hence, hang not on my garments.
MIRANDA   Sir, have pity;
    I'll be his surety.
PROSPERO   Silence! one word more
    Shall make me chide thee, if not hate thee. What,
    An advocate for an impostor? Hush!   480
    Thou think'st there is no more such shapes as
      he,
    Having seen but him and Caliban; foolish
      wench,
    To the most of men, this is a Caliban,
    And they to him are angels.
MIRANDA   My affections
    Are then most humble; I have no ambition
    To see a goodlier man.
PROSPERO   Come on, obey.
    Thy nerves are in their infancy again,
    And have no vigour in them.
FERDINAND   So they are.
    My spirits, as in a dream, are all bound up;
    My father's loss, the weakness which I feel,   490
    The wrack of all my friends, nor this man's
      threats
    To whom I am subdued, are but light to me,
    Might I but through my prison once a day
    Behold this maid: all corners else o' th' earth
    Let liberty make use of; space enough
    Have I in such a prison.
PROSPERO [*Aside*]   It works. [*To* FERDINAND]
    Come on.
    [*To* ARIEL] Thou hast done well, fine Ariel.
      Follow me;
    Hark what thou else shalt do me.
MIRANDA   Be of comfort;
    My father's of a better nature, sir,

500–1   This . . . him *His recent behaviour is not according to his usual custom*

503   points *details*

Than he appears by speech. This is unwonted 500
       Which now came from him.
PROSPERO [*To* ARIEL]   Thou shalt be as free
       As mountain winds; but then exactly do
       All points of my command.
ARIEL   To the syllable.
PROSPERO [*To* FERDINAND] Come, follow. [*To* MIRANDA]
       Speak not for him.

                                        [*Exeunt*

ACT TWO, scene 1

We now get a closer look at the royal party, whom we saw only fleetingly through the confusion of the storm in Act one scene 1. Their separate characters now emerge much more clearly. At the beginning Sebastian and Anthonio will be standing somewhat apart, commenting sarcastically on Gonzalo's attempts to comfort Alonso. Anthonio is noticeably un-dukelike, by the standards of Shakespeare's time, in allowing Sebastian, his subordinate, such familiarity with him.

3	Is . . . loss *Is a mercy that far outweighs the loss we have suffered.*
	hint *occasion*
5	The masters . . . the merchant *The officers of some trading vessel and the merchant who owns her*
6	theme of woe *subject for lamentation*
	for *as for*
9	with *against*
10–11	like cold porridge *i.e. as something unattractive. There is also a pun, Alonso's request for 'peace' suggesting pease porridge.*
12	visitor *spiritual comforter*
13	give him o'er *so let him go so easily*
14–15	winding . . . wit *making laborious preparations for a striking remark*
17	One *The 'watch of his wit' has struck one.*
	Tell *Keep count of its strokes.*
18–19	When . . . entertainer – *If we feel miserable whenever an occasion for misery occurs, we receive –*
20	A dollar *Sebastian cuts short Gonzalo's pious remark by deliberately misunderstanding* entertainer. *He takes it to mean not 'the one who accepts' but 'performer', and suggests that the latter's reward is money.*
21	Dolour *Grief. Gonzalo caps Sebastian's pun with another.*
23	You . . . wiselier *You have given a more intelligent interpretation of what I said*
26	Fie . . . tongue *From here down to line 83 (' "Widow Dido", said you?') Anthonio and Sebastian are once more talking aside to each other, though sometimes perhaps loudly enough for the others to hear them.*

ACT TWO

Scene 1. *Enter* ALONSO, SEBASTIAN, ANTHONIO, GONZALO,
ADRIAN, FRANCISCO, *and other* COURTIERS

GONZALO Beseech you, sir, be merry; you have cause
    (So have we all) of joy; for our escape
    Is much beyond our loss. Our hint of woe
    Is common; every day, some sailor's wife,
    The masters of some merchant, and the
      merchant
    Have just our theme of woe; but for the miracle –
    I mean our preservation – few in millions
    Can speak like us. Then wisely, good sir, weigh
    Our sorrow with our comfort.
ALONSO   Prithee, peace.
SEBASTIAN [*Aside to* ANTHONIO] He receives comfort like   10
cold porridge.
ANTHONIO [*Aside to* SEBASTIAN] The visitor will not
give him o'er so.
SEBASTIAN [*Aside to* ANTHONIO] Look, he's winding up
the watch of his wit; by and by it will strike.
GONZALO Sir –
SEBASTIAN [*Aside to* ANTHONIO] One. Tell.
GONZALO When every grief is entertained that's
    offered,
    Comes to th'entertainer –
SEBASTIAN A dollar.   20
GONZALO Dolour comes to him indeed; you have spoken
truer than you purposed.
SEBASTIAN You have taken it wiselier than I meant you
should.
GONZALO Therefore, my Lord –
ANTHONIO Fie, what a spendthrift is he of his
    tongue.
ALONSO I prithee, spare.
GONZALO   Well, I have done. But yet –

Which . . . crow? *Which of the two do you bet will be the first to speak, he or Adrian?*

33 wager *stake*

34 A laughter *They have lost all their possessions in the shipwreck, so the only reward for the winner will be the laughter to be gained from the joke.*

35 A match *Agreed*

38 So, you're paid *Anthonio has won the bet, and, by laughing, received his winnings.*

42 He could not miss 't *Adrian couldn't have failed to say 'Yet –'*

43–4 delicate temperance *delightful climate*

45 Temperance . . . wench *Anthonio takes* Temperance, *in the sense of 'moderation', to be a girl's name, and perhaps gives* delicate *its Elizabethan sense of 'self-indulgent'. Thus* delicate temperance *becomes an absurd contradiction in terms.*

54 lush and lusty *luxuriant and vigorous*

57 eye *spot*

61 credit *belief*

62 vouched *guaranteed*

74

SEBASTIAN He will be talking.

ANTHONIO Which, of he or Adrian, for a good wager, first begins to crow? 30

SEBASTIAN The old cock.

ANTHONIO The cockerel.

SEBASTIAN Done: the wager?

ANTHONIO A laughter.

SEBASTIAN A match.

ADRIAN Though this island seem to be desert –

ANTHONIO Ha, ha, ha!

SEBASTIAN So, you're paid.

ADRIAN Uninhabitable, and almost inaccessible –

SEBASTIAN Yet – 40

ADRIAN Yet –

ANTHONIO He could not miss 't.

ADRIAN It must needs be of subtle, tender, and delicate temperance.

ANTHONIO Temperance was a delicate wench.

SEBASTIAN Ay, and a subtle, as he most learnedly delivered.

ADRIAN The air breathes upon us here most sweetly.

SEBASTIAN As if it had lungs, and rotten ones.

ANTHONIO Or as 'twere perfumed by a fen. 50

GONZALO Here is everything advantageous to life.

ANTHONIO True, save means to live.

SEBASTIAN Of that there's none, or little.

GONZALO How lush and lusty the grass looks! How green!

ANTHONIO The ground indeed is tawny.

SEBASTIAN With an eye of green in 't.

ANTHONIO He misses not much.

SEBASTIAN No, he doth but mistake the truth totally.

GONZALO But the rarity of it is, which is indeed almost 60 beyond credit –

SEBASTIAN As many vouched rarities are.

GONZALO That our garments, being – as they were – drenched in the sea, hold notwithstanding their

75

69   pocket up his report *suppress what he says*

74–5   'Twas . . . return *Said ironically.*

77   to *as*

79   Widow? *Dido, in Virgil's Aeneid, was in fact a widow,
            but she was usually thought of rather as Aeneas's
            mistress; hence Anthonio's surprise. The following
            series of jokes about Dido is no doubt intended to be
            silly, and thus to indicate the triviality of Anthonio
            and his follower.*

81   widower Aeneas *Aeneas was a widower according to the
            Aeneid, but, like Dido, was better known as a lover.*

82   how you take it! *what a fuss you are making about it!*

83–4   make me study of that *puzzle me by saying that*

88–90   His word . . . houses too *Amphion had a miraculous
            harp, which caused the walls of Thebes to rise.
            Gonzalo's mistaken identification of Tunis with
            Carthage (which was completely destroyed by the
            Romans) performs an even greater miracle, by resur-
            recting a whole city.*

95   kernels *pips*

98   in good time *that's right (ironic)*

freshness and glosses, being rather new-dyed than stained with salt water.

ANTHONIO If but one of his pockets could speak, would it not say he lies?

SEBASTIAN Ay, or very falsely pocket up his report.

GONZALO Methinks our garments are now as fresh as when we put them on first in Afric, at the marriage of the King's fair daughter Claribel to the King of Tunis.

SEBASTIAN 'Twas a sweet marriage, and we prosper well in our return.

ADRIAN Tunis was never graced before with such a paragon to their queen.

GONZALO Not since widow Dido's time.

ANTHONIO Widow? A pox o' that. How came that widow in? Widow Dido!

SEBASTIAN What if he had said 'widower Aeneas' too? Good Lord, how you take it!

ADRIAN 'Widow Dido,' said you? You make me study of that; she was of Carthage, not of Tunis.

GONZALO This Tunis, sir, was Carthage.

ADRIAN Carthage?

GONZALO I assure you, Carthage.

ANTHONIO His word is more than the miraculous harp.

SEBASTIAN He hath raised the wall, and houses too.

ANTHONIO What impossible matter will he make easy next?

SEBASTIAN I think he will carry this island home in his pocket, and give it his son for an apple.

ANTHONIO And sowing the kernels of it in the sea, bring forth more islands.

GONZALO Ay.

ANTHONIO Why, in good time.

GONZALO Sir, we were talking, that our garments seem now as fresh as when we were at Tunis at the marriage of your daughter, who is now Queen.

103   Bate, I beseech you *I beg you to make an exception of*

106   in a sort *in a manner of speaking*

109–10   against . . . sense *despite my mind's lack of appetite for them*

112   rate *opinion*

117–25   I saw . . . to land *This description has an almost emblematic formality. Francisco offers not a realistic account of what he saw, but a powerfully stylized image of triumph over adversity.*

119   breasted . . . him *fought his way over the hugest wave he met*

121   oared *rowed (swimming being compared to rowing)*

123–4   that . . . As *which bowed down over its own foot, eaten away by the waves, as if*

126   Sir *Sebastian, having been standing aside exchanging comments with Anthonio, now intervenes directly in the conversation with the King.*

128   loose . . . to *mate her with (a deliberately crude way of putting it, as if they were animals)*

129   at least *to say the least. (If not lost completely, as Alonso has just said, she is at least banished.)*

130   Who . . . on't *Who has good cause (by being so unhappily married) to make you weep on her account (rather than on your own, at having lost her)*

ANTHONIO And the rarest that e'er came there.

SEBASTIAN Bate, I beseech you, widow Dido.

ANTHONIO O, widow Dido! Ay, widow Dido.

GONZALO Is not, sir, my doublet as fresh as the first day
  I wore it? I mean in a sort.

ANTHONIO That sort was well fished for.

GONZALO When I wore it at your daughter's marriage.

ALONSO You cram these words into mine ears against
    The stomach of my sense. Would I had never 110
    Married my daughter there, for coming thence
    My son is lost, and, in my rate, she too,
    Who is so far from Italy removed,
    I ne'er again shall see her. O thou mine heir
    Of Naples and of Milan, what strange fish
    Hath made his meal on thee?

FRANCISCO   Sir, he may live.
    I saw him beat the surges under him,
    And ride upon their backs; he trod the water,
    Whose enmity he flung aside, and breasted
    The surge most swoln that met him; his bold
     head   120
    'Bove the contentious waves he kept, and oared
    Himself with his good arms in lusty stroke
    To the shore, that o'er his wave-worn basis
     bowed,
    As stooping to relieve him. I not doubt
    He came alive to land.

ALONSO   No, no, he's gone.

SEBASTIAN Sir, you may thank yourself for this great
    loss,
    That would not bless our Europe with your
     daughter,
    But rather loose her to an African,
    Where she, at least, is banished from your
     eye,
    Who hath cause to wet the grief on't.

ALONSO   Prithee, peace. 130

131	importuned otherwise *begged to do otherwise*
133-4	Weighed . . . bow *Was equally balanced between her obedience to you and her reluctance to marry a negro*
136-7	Mo . . . comfort them *more women made widows by the present disaster than the number of men who will get safely back to console them*
138	dear'st *most painful part*
140	time *a suitable time*
142	chirurgeonly *spoken like a good surgeon*
144	Fowl weather *Another silly pun.*
145	plantation *colonisation. In the next line, Anthonio takes the word to mean 'planting'.*
146	nettle . . . docks . . . mallows *Three weeds.*
148	'Scape *avoid. As we learn later, Stephano has the only wine that has survived the shipwreck.*
149	commonwealth *state*
	by contraries . . . things *organise everything in a way contrary to what is usual*
150	traffic *trade*
151	admit *permit*
152	Letters *Literacy*
153	service *servants*
	succession *inheritance of property*
154	Bourn . . . land *Boundary or limit of land (i.e. he would not permit land to be held as private property).*
	tilth *agriculture*

SEBASTIAN You were kneeled to and importuned other-
          wise
          By all of us; and the fair soul herself
          Weighed between loathness and obedience, at
          Which end o' the beam should bow. We have
              lost your son,
          I fear for ever; Milan and Naples have
          Mo widows in them of this business' making
          Than we bring men to comfort them. The fault's
              your own.
ALONSO So is the dear'st o' the loss.
GONZALO   My lord Sebastian,
          The truth you speak doth lack some
              gentleness,
          And time to speak it in. You rub the sore   140
          When you should bring the plaster.
SEBASTIAN   Very well.
ANTHONIO And most chirurgeonly.
GONZALO It is foul weather in us all, good sir,
          When you are cloudy.
SEBASTIAN   Fowl weather?
ANTHONIO   Very foul.
GONZALO Had I plantation of this isle, my lord –
ANTHONIO He'd sow 't with nettle-seed.
SEBASTIAN   Or docks, or mallows.
GONZALO And were the king on't, what would I do?
SEBASTIAN 'Scape being drunk, for want of wine.
GONZALO I' the commonwealth I would by contraries
          Execute all things; for no kind of traffic   150
          Would I admit; no name of magistrate;
          Letters should not be known; riches, poverty,
          And use of service, none; contract, succession,
          Bourn, bound of land, tilth, vineyard, none;
          No use of metal, corn, or wine, or oil;
          No occupation, all men idle, all;
          And women too, but innocent and pure;
          No sovereignty –

SEBASTIAN   Yet he would be king on't.

ANTHONIO The latter end of his commonwealth forgets
the beginning.   160

GONZALO All things in common Nature should produce
    Without sweat or endeavour; treason, felony,
    Sword, pike, knife, gun, or need of any
      engine
    Would I not have; but Nature should bring
      forth
    Of it own kind all foison, all abundance,
    To feed my innocent people.

SEBASTIAN No marrying 'mong his subjects?

ANTHONIO None, man, all idle; whores and knaves.

GONZALO I would with such perfection govern, sir,
    T'excel the Golden Age.

SEBASTIAN   'Save his Majesty!   170

ANTHONIO Long live Gonzalo!

GONZALO   And – do you mark me, sir?

ALONSO Prithee, no more; thou dost talk nothing to
me.

GONZALO I do well believe your Highness, and did it to
minister occasion to these gentlemen, who are of such
sensible and nimble lungs, that they always use to
laugh at nothing.

ANTHONIO 'Twas you we laughed at.

GONZALO Who in this kind of merry fooling am nothing
to you: so you may continue, and laugh at nothing
still.   180

ANTHONIO What a blow was there given!

SEBASTIAN And it had not fallen flat-long.

GONZALO You are gentlemen of brave mettle; you would
lift the moon out of her sphere if she would continue
in it five weeks without changing.

    Enter ARIEL, *invisible, playing solemn music*

SEBASTIAN We would so, and then go a bat-fowling.

ANTHONIO Nay, good my lord, be not angry.

GONZALO No, I warrant you, I will not adventure my

190   heavy *drowsy. It is of course the magic charm represented
         by Ariel's music that sends all but Anthonio and
         Sebastian to sleep.*

193   with . . . up *by shutting in sleep, blot out*

195   omit . . . it *try to avoid the drowsy onset of sleep*

203   nimble *lively*
204   as by consent *as if they had made an agreement to do so*

208   th'occasion speaks thee *the opportunity beckons to you*

discretion so weakly. Will you laugh me asleep, for I
am very heavy?   190
ANTHONIO Go sleep, and hear us.

All sleep except ALONSO, SEBASTIAN *and* ANTHONIO

ALONSO What, all so soon asleep? I wish mine eyes
    Would, with themselves, shut up my thoughts.
     I find
    They are inclined to do so.
SEBASTIAN   Please you, sir,
    Do not omit the heavy offer of it.
    It seldom visits sorrow; when it doth,
    It is a comforter.
ANTHONIO   We two, my lord,
    Will guard your person while you take your
     rest,
    And watch your safety.
ALONSO   Thank you. Wondrous heavy . . .
        ALONSO *falls asleep.*

                    [*Exit* ARIEL

SEBASTIAN What a strange drowsiness possesses them! 200
ANTHONIO It is the quality o' the climate.
SEBASTIAN   Why
    Doth it not then our eyelids sink? I find not
    Myself disposed to sleep.
ANTHONIO   Nor I; my spirits are nimble.
    They fell together all, as by consent;
    They dropped, as by a thunder-stroke. What
     might,
    Worthy Sebastian . . .? O, what might . . .? No
     more.
    And yet methinks I see it in thy face,
    What thou shouldst be: th'occasion speaks thee,
     and
    My strong imagination sees a crown
    Dropping upon thy head.
SEBASTIAN   What? Art thou waking? 210
ANTHONIO Do you not hear me speak?

212–13	thou ... sleep *what you say is the product of a sleeping mind*
217–18	wink'st ... waking *you are shutting your eyes (to opportunity) even though you are awake*
218	distinctly *intelligibly*
221–2	if ... o'er *if you pay attention to what I say; and if you do so, you will be three times the man you are now*
222	standing water *water flowing neither one way nor the other (i.e. open to any suggestion)*
223	flow *i.e. make a decisive move* ebb *i.e. keep in the background*
224	Hereditary sloth *The laziness appropriate to the position I am born to (i.e. that of a king's younger brother, who must keep his ambitions in check)*
225–7	If ... invest it *If you only knew how near you come to the purpose I have in mind by thus referring mockingly to your status as a younger brother; and how, in seeming to strip it of honour, you only confer greater honour on it. (Sebastian has invested his position in robes of state by alluding to his nearness to the throne; in the event of his brother's death, he would have a good claim to succeed.)*
228	bottom *i.e. of the stream; that is, distance from greatness and power*
230–2	The setting ... yield *The fixed expression on your face declares that you have something important to say – a new idea to which you can give expression only with a struggle*
234	shall ... memory *A pun: both 'shall be as forgetful' and 'shall be as little remembered'.*
235	earthed *buried*
236–7	he's ... persuade *he is the very essence of persuasiveness, his only profession is to persuade. (Anthonio is referring to Gonzalo, who has been trying to comfort Alonso, and whose bad memory showed itself when he said that if he were king of the island there would be no sovereignty.)*

SEBASTIAN   I do, and surely
          It is a sleepy language, and thou speak'st
          Out of thy sleep. What is it thou didst say?
          This is a strange repose, to be asleep
          With eyes wide open; standing, speaking,
              moving,
          And yet so fast asleep.
ANTHONIO   Noble Sebastian,
          Thou let'st thy fortune sleep – die rather;
              wink'st
          Whiles thou art waking.
SEBASTIAN   Thou dost snore distinctly:
          There's meaning in thy snores.
ANTHONIO I am more serious than my custom: you   220
          Must be so too, if heed me; which to do,
          Trebles thee o'er.
SEBASTIAN   Well, I am standing water.
ANTHONIO I'll teach you how to flow.
SEBASTIAN   Do so. To ebb
          Hereditary sloth instructs me.
ANTHONIO   O,
          If you but knew how you the purpose cherish
          Whiles thus you mock it; how in stripping it
          You more invest it. Ebbing men, indeed,
          Most often do so near the bottom run
          By their own fear or sloth.
SEBASTIAN   Prithee say on.
          The setting of thine eye and cheek proclaim   230
          A matter from thee; and a birth indeed
          Which throes thee much to yield.
ANTHONIO   Thus, sir:
          Although this lord of weak remembrance,
              this
          Who shall be of as little memory
          When he is earthed, hath here almost
              persuaded –
          For he's a spirit of persuasion, only

238–9   'Tis . . . swims *It is as impossible that Ferdinand is not drowned as that Alonso, whom we see asleep before us, is really swimming*

241   that way *in that respect*

243–4   Ambition . . . there *Ambition itself cannot see further than the hope of a crown, and indeed must doubt that it can see even that*

247–8   she that dwells . . . life *she who lives so far away that it would take a lifetime to get within thirty miles of her*

248   note *news*
post *messenger*

250–1   till . . . razorable *until boys born at the moment of sending her the news had grown old enough to have beards*

251   she that from whom *she on our return journey from whom*

252   cast *vomited up by the sea (i.e. cast ashore). Cast also means 'given a part', and this pun introduces a series of other theatrical images in the next few lines (perform . . . act . . . prologue . . . discharge).*

255   discharge *acting of a part*

258   cubit *about twenty inches*
260   us *i.e. the cubits*
260–1   Keep . . . wake *You stay in Tunis, Claribel, and let Sebastian trouble himself about Naples*

Professes to persuade – the King his son's alive,
'Tis as impossible that he's undrowned
As he that sleeps here, swims.
SEBASTIAN   I have no hope
That he's undrowned.
ANTHONIO   O, out of that no hope, 240
What great hope have you? No hope that way
is
Another way so high a hope that even
Ambition cannot pierce a wink beyond,
But doubt discovery there. Will you grant with
me
That Ferdinand is drowned?
SEBASTIAN   He's gone.
ANTHONIO   Then tell me,
Who's the next heir of Naples?
SEBASTIAN   Claribel.
ANTHONIO She that is Queen of Tunis; she that dwells
Ten leagues beyond man's life; she that from
Naples
Can have no note, unless the sun were post –
The man i' the moon's too slow – till new-born
chins   250
Be rough and razorable; she that from whom
We all were sea-swallowed, though some cast
again,
And that by destiny, to perform an act
Whereof what's past is prologue; what to come
In yours and my discharge.
SEBASTIAN   What stuff is this? How say you?
'Tis true my brother's daughter's Queen of
Tunis;
So is she heir of Naples; 'twixt which regions
There is some space.
ANTHONIO   A space whose every cubit
Seems to cry out, 'How shall that Claribel
Measure us back to Naples? Keep in Tunis,   260

263   There be that *There are those who*

266–7   I ... chat *I could be a chattering bird with as much power to make profound speeches as Gonzalo. (Birds such as jackdaws can be taught to repeat a few words, though, of course, without understanding them.)*

267–8   O ... I do! *If only you had the purpose in mind that I have!*

270–1   And ... fortune *And how contentedly do you regard this prospect of good fortune?*

273   sit upon *fit. Clothes, the outward sign of the roles people play (as ruler, nobleman, magician, or jester), form an important verbal and dramatic image in this most theatrical of Shakespeare's plays.*

274   feater *more neatly*

275   fellows *equals*
           men *subordinates*

277–8   If ... slipper *If my conscience were a chilblain, it would make me wear a slipper (i.e. if it caused me even slight physical pain, then it would hinder my activity – but it doesn't).*

279–81   twenty ... molest *if conscience were all that prevented me from becoming Duke of Milan, twenty consciences might melt away like sweets before they did me any harm*

280   candied *sugared*

283   that's *that is to say*

284   steel *i.e. dagger or sword*

285–6   whiles ... morsel *meanwhile you, doing similarly, might put this old remnant of a Gonzalo to sleep for ever*

And let Sebastian wake.' Say this were death
That now hath seized them, why, they were no
    worse
Than now they are. There be that can rule
    Naples
As well as he that sleeps; lords that can prate
As amply and unnecessarily
As this Gonzalo; I myself could make
A chough of as deep chat. O, that you bore
The mind that I do! What a sleep were this
For your advancement! Do you understand me?
SEBASTIAN Methinks I do.
ANTHONIO   And how does your content 270
    Tender your own good fortune?
SEBASTIAN   I remember
    You did supplant your brother Prospero.
ANTHONIO   True;
    And look how well my garments sit upon me,
    Much feater than before; my brother's servants
    Were then my fellows, now they are my men.
SEBASTIAN But for your conscience.
ANTHONIO Ay, sir: where lies that? If 'twere a kibe
    'Twould put me to my slipper; but I feel not
    This deity in my bosom; twenty consciences
    That stand 'twixt me and Milan, candied be
        they,   280
    And melt, ere they molest. Here lies your
        brother,
    No better than the earth he lies upon,
    If he were that which now he's like, that's dead;
    Whom I, with this obedient steel, three inches
        of it,
    Can lay to bed for ever; whiles you, doing thus,
    To the perpetual wink for aye might put
    This ancient morsel, this Sir Prudence, who
    Should not upbraid our course. For all the
        rest,

289	take ... as *accept our explanations as eagerly as*
290–1	tell ... hour *agree that the time is right for any course of action that we say is appropriate*
291–2	Thy ... precedent *I will follow your example.* (Case and precedent *are both legal terms.*)

295	Draw together *Let us draw our swords at the same moment*
297	fall it *let it fall*

300	else ... dies *otherwise his plan will fail*

303	His ... take *Is acting at leisure*

307	sudden *prompt in acting*

311	securing *guarding*
313	or rather lions *It suddenly occurs to him that lions would be more likely, and more dangerous, inhabitants of a desert island.*

They'll take suggestion as a cat laps milk;
They'll tell the clock to any business that   290
We say befits the hour.

SEBASTIAN   Thy case, dear friend,
Shall be my precedent; as thou got'st Milan,
I'll come by Naples. Draw thy sword, one stroke
Shall free thee from the tribute which thou
payest,
And I, the King, shall love thee.

ANTHONIO   Draw together;
And when I rear my hand, do you the like,
To fall it on Gonzalo.

SEBASTIAN   O, but one word.

He takes ANTHONIO *aside to talk. Enter* ARIEL *with
music and song*

ARIEL My master through his Art foresees the danger
That you, his friend, are in, and sends me forth –
For else his project dies – to keep them living. 300

ARIEL *sings in* GONZALO's *ear*

While you here do snoring lie,
Open-eyed Conspiracy
His time doth take.
If of life you keep a care,
Shake off slumber and beware:
Awake, awake!

ANTHONIO [*To* SEBASTIAN] Then let us both be sudden.

GONZALO [*Waking, and rousing* ALONSO] Now good
angels preserve the King!   [*The others wake*

ALONSO Why, how now, hoa; awake? Why are you
drawn?
Wherefore this ghastly looking?

GONZALO   What's the matter? 310

SEBASTIAN Whiles we stood here securing your repose,
Even now, we heard a hollow burst of bellowing,
Like bulls, or rather lions; did't not wake you?
It struck mine ear most terribly.

ALONSO   I heard nothing.

93

316–17   sure . . . lions *Anthonio enthusiastically backs up the more plausible of Sebastian's lies.*

322   verily *for certain*

ACT TWO, scene 2

2   flats *flat places, hence likely to be marshy and unhealthy*

3   By inch-meal *Inch by inch*
4   nor *neither*

5   urchin-shows *displays of goblins*

6   firebrand *will-o'-the-wisp*

9   mow *grin*

ANTHONIO O, 'twas a din to fright a monster's ear,
To make an earthquake; sure it was the roar
Of a whole herd of lions.

ALONSO   Heard you this, Gonzalo?

GONZALO Upon mine honour, sir, I heard a humming,
And that a strange one too, which did awake me.
I shaked you, sir, and cried; as mine eyes opened, 320
I saw their weapons drawn. There was a noise,
That's verily. 'Tis best we stand upon our guard,
Or that we quit this place; let's draw our
weapons.

ALONSO Lead off this ground, and let's make further
search
For my poor son.

GONZALO   Heavens keep him from these beasts,
For he is sure i' th' island.

ALONSO   Lead away.

ARIEL Prospero my lord shall know what I have done.
So, King, go safely on to seek thy son.   [*Exeunt*

Scene 2. *Enter* CALIBAN *with a burden of wood. A noise of
thunder heard*

CALIBAN All the infections that the sun sucks up
From bogs, fens, flats, on Prosper fall, and
make him
By inch-meal a disease. His spirits hear me,
And yet I needs must curse. But they'll nor
pinch,
Fright me with urchin-shows, pitch me i' the
mire,
Nor lead me like a firebrand in the dark
Out of my way, unless he bid 'em; but
For every trifle are they set upon me;
Sometime like apes, that mow and chatter at
me,
And after bite me; then like hedgehogs, which 10

11–12	mount . . . pricks *raise their prickles*
13	wound *twined about*
14	madness *The* ss *of* madness *continues the hissing noise*
17	mind *notice*
18	bear off *shield one from*
21	bombard *great leather jug for drink. Thus we are put in the right frame of mind for the drunken Stephano's entrance.*
27	poor-John *dried hake*
28	England *The audiences of Shakespeare's time seem to have enjoyed such jokes against their own country; there is a similar one in* Hamlet.
29	painted *advertised by a painted sign at a fair*
31	make a man *make its owner's fortune*
32	doit *small coin*
34	Indian *Native of America or the West Indies. Such natives were frequently exhibited in England in Shakespeare's time.*
35–6	let . . . longer *express my opinion and no longer conceal it*
37	suffered *been killed*
39	gaberdine *cloak*
41	shroud *wrap myself up*
	dregs *Thus the image of drink is repeated as Stephano comes in with his bottle.*

96

Lie tumbling in my barefoot way, and mount
Their pricks at my footfall; sometime am I
All wound with adders, who with cloven tongues
Do hiss me into madness.

Enter TRINCULO

Lo, now, lo!
Here comes a spirit of his, and to torment
me
For bringing wood in slowly. I'll fall flat;
Perchance he will not mind me.

TRINCULO Here's neither bush nor shrub to bear off any
weather at all. And another storm brewing; I hear
it sing i' the wind. Yond same black cloud, yond   20
huge one, looks like a foul bombard that would shed
his liquor. If it should thunder as it did before, I
know not where to hide my head: yond same cloud
cannot choose but fall by pailfuls. [*Notices* CALIBAN]
What have we here, a man or a fish? Dead or alive?
A fish, he smells like a fish; a very ancient and fish-
like smell; a kind of . . . not of the newest poor-John;
a strange fish. Were I in England now, as once
I was, and had but this fish painted, not a holiday fool
there but would give a piece of silver. There would   30
this monster make a man; any strange beast there
makes a man; when they will not give a doit to relieve
a lame beggar, they will lay out ten to see a dead
Indian. Legged like a man, and his fins like arms;
[*Feels* CALIBAN] warm o' my troth! I do now let loose
my opinion, hold it no longer: this is no fish, but an
islander that hath lately suffered by a thunderbolt.
[*More thunder*] Alas, the storm is come again. My
best way is to creep under his gaberdine; there is no
other shelter hereabout. Misery acquaints a man with   40
strange bedfellows; I will here shroud till the dregs of
the storm be past.

He hides under CALIBAN's *cloak. Enter* STEPHANO
singing, with a bottle

45   This . . . funeral *Stephano has already drunk enough to speak of his own likely death less seriously than one might expect.*
scurvy *worthless*
47   swabber *sailor whose job it was to clean the ship.*

59   men of Ind *Indians (meaning as in line 34 above).*

61–3   As proper . . . ground *As fine a man as ever went on crutches cannot make him give way (said ironically)*

67   ague *acute fever (which would make one groan and shiver)*

69   recover *cure*

71–2   trod . . . leather *wore shoes*

STEPHANO   I shall no more to sea, to sea,
             Here shall I die ashore –
This is a very scurvy tune to sing at a man's funeral;
well, here's my comfort.

     He drinks from his bottle, then sings
    The master, the swabber, the boatswain and I,
       The gunner and his mate,
    Loved Mall, Meg, and Marian, and Margery,
       But none of us cared for Kate;   50
       For she had a tongue with a tang,
       Would cry to a sailor, 'Go hang!'
    She loved not the savour of tar nor of pitch,
    Yet a tailor might scratch her where'er she did
      itch.
    Then to sea, boys, and let her go hang.
This is a scurvy tune too; but here's my comfort.

                                   [*Drinks*

CALIBAN Do not torment me. O!

STEPHANO What's the matter? Have we devils here? Do
you put tricks upon's with savages and men of Ind?
ha? I have not 'scaped drowning, to be afeard now 60
of your four legs; for it hath been said, 'As proper a
man as ever went on four legs cannot make him give
ground;' and it shall be said so again, while Stephano
breathes at nostrils.

CALIBAN The spirit torments me. O!

STEPHANO This is some monster of the isle with four
legs, who hath got, as I take it, an ague. Where the
devil should he learn our language? I will give him
some relief, if it be but for that. If I can recover him,
and keep him tame, and get to Naples with him, he's 70
a present for any emperor that ever trod on neat's-
leather.

CALIBAN Do not torment me, prithee; I'll bring my wood
home faster.

STEPHANO He's in his fit now, and does not talk after the
wisest. He shall taste of my bottle: if he have never

78–80   **I will . . . soundly** *even too much will be too low a price for him: the man who buys him will have to pay an enormous amount*

82   **trembling** *Caliban thinks that Trinculo's trembling, caused by terror, is that of a spirit being forced by Prospero's magic to torment him.*

84   **Come . . . ways** *come along now*

85   **cat** *There was a proverb that strong drink would make even a cat talk.*

86   **shake** *shake off*

87   **and that soundly** *and thoroughly, too*

88   **chaps** *jaws*

92   **delicate** *ingeniously constructed*

101   **I . . . spoon** *The proverb is that 'He that sups with the devil must have a long spoon'.*

108   **siege** *excrement*

            moon-calf *shapeless monstrosity; idiot*

109   **vent** *excrete*

drunk wine afore, it will go near to remove his fit.
If I can recover him, and keep him tame, I will not
take too much for him; he shall pay for him that hath
him, and that soundly.   80

CALIBAN Thou dost me yet but little hurt; thou wilt
anon, I know it by thy trembling; now Prosper works
upon thee.

STEPHANO Come on your ways; open your mouth; here
is that which will give language to you, cat. Open
your mouth; this will shake your shaking, I can tell
you, and that soundly. You cannot tell who's your
friend; open your chaps again.

TRINCULO I should know that voice: it should be –
but he is drowned; and these are devils. O defend   90
me!

STEPHANO Four legs and two voices; a most delicate
monster! His forward voice, now, is to speak well of
his friend; his backward voice is to utter foul speeches
and to detract. If all the wine in my bottle will recover him, I will help his ague. Come. Amen! I will
pour some in thy other mouth.

TRINCULO Stephano!

STEPHANO Doth thy other mouth call me? Mercy,
mercy! This is a devil, and no monster: I will leave   100
him, I have no long spoon.

TRINCULO Stephano! If thou beest Stephano, touch me,
and speak to me, for I am Trinculo. Be not afeard:
thy good friend Trinculo.

STEPHANO If thou beest Trinculo, come forth; I'll pull
thee by the lesser legs; if any be Trinculo's legs,
these are they. Thou art very Trinculo indeed! How
cam'st thou to be the siege of this moon-calf? Can he
vent Trinculos?

TRINCULO I took him to be killed with a thunderstroke. 110
But art thou not drowned, Stephano? I hope now thou
art not drowned. Is the storm over-blown? I hid me
under the dead moon-calf's gaberdine, for fear of

116   turn me about *In his joy, Trinculo has been making Stephano dance round with him.*

117   constant *settled*

118   and if *if*

123   butt of sack *cask of white wine*

132   kiss the book *i.e. drink from the bottle. He pretends that it is a Bible, on which Trinculo must take an oath.*

140   when time was *once upon a time*

142–3   and . . . bush *The man in the moon was supposed to have been banished there for gathering brushwood with his dog on a Sunday, and people imagined they could see him there with his dog and sticks.*

149   drawn *drunk*

102

the storm. And art thou living, Stephano? O Stephano, two Neapolitans 'scaped?

STEPHANO Prithee do not turn me about, my stomach is not constant.

CALIBAN [*Aside*] These be fine things, and if they be not sprites. That's a brave god, and bears celestial liquor. I will kneel to him.   120

STEPHANO How didst thou 'scape? How cam'st thou hither? Swear by this bottle how thou cam'st hither. I escaped upon a butt of sack, which the sailors heaved o'erboard, by this bottle (which I made of the bark of a tree with mine own hands, since I was cast ashore).

CALIBAN I'll swear upon that bottle to be thy true subject, for the liquor is not earthly.

STEPHANO Here; swear then how thou escapedst.

TRINCULO Swum ashore, man, like a duck: I can swim 130 like a duck, I'll be sworn.

STEPHANO Here, kiss the book. Though thou canst swim like a duck, thou art made like a goose.

TRINCULO O Stephano, hast any more of this?

STEPHANO The whole butt, man; my cellar is in a rock by the sea-side, where my wine is hid. How now, moon-calf, how does thine ague?

CALIBAN Hast thou not dropped from heaven?

STEPHANO Out o' the moon, I do assure thee. I was the man i' the moon, when time was.   140

CALIBAN I have seen thee in her, and I do adore thee; my mistress showed me thee, and thy dog, and thy bush.

STEPHANO Come, swear to that: kiss the book.
    He gives CALIBAN *the bottle to drink*
I will furnish it anon with new contents. Swear!

TRINCULO By this good light, this is a very shallow monster; I afeard of him? A very weak monster! the man i' the moon! A most poor credulous monster! Well drawn, monster, in good sooth!

150   I'll . . . island *Twelve years before, Caliban must have done this for Prospero; and he feels that Prospero has not justly rewarded him. Now the same thing is going to happen again, under the influence of drink supplied by new colonists much less noble than Prospero. The scene is comic, of course; but it stands, too, as an almost despairing satire on the selfishness of colonists and the folly of natives.*

152   perfidious *For the reason explained in the next sentence: Caliban is so fond of the drink that he would steal it from the 'god' who owns it, given the opportunity.*

169   crabs *crab apples*

170   pig-nuts *earth-nuts*

174   scamels *A kind of bird (?). The word is obscure; an emendation that has been suggested is* sea-mells *(i.e. sea-mews).*

177   we . . . here *Thus Stephano, Trinculo and Caliban provide a comic parallel to the plots of Sebastian and Anthonio seen in the last scene.*

CALIBAN I'll show thee every fertile inch o' th' island; 150
And I will kiss thy foot. I prithee, be my god.

TRINCULO By this light, a most perfidious and drunken
monster! When's god's asleep, he'll rob his bottle.

CALIBAN I'll kiss thy foot. I'll swear myself thy subject.

STEPHANO Come on, then; down and swear.

TRINCULO I shall laugh myself to death at this puppy-
headed monster: a most scurvy monster! I could find
in my heart to beat him –

STEPHANO Come, kiss.

TRINCULO – but that the poor monster's in drink. An 160
abominable monster!

CALIBAN I'll show thee the best springs; I'll pluck thee
berries;
I'll fish for thee; and get thee wood enough.
A plague upon the tyrant that I serve!
I'll bear him no more sticks, but follow thee,
Thou wondrous man.

TRINCULO A most ridiculous monster, to make a wonder
of a poor drunkard.

CALIBAN I prithee let me bring thee where crabs
grow;
And I with my long nails will dig thee pig-nuts; 170
Show thee a jay's nest, and instruct thee how
To snare the nimble marmoset; I'll bring thee
To clustering filberts, and sometimes I'll get
thee
Young scamels from the rock. Wilt thou go with
me?

STEPHANO I prithee now, lead the way without any
more talking. Trinculo, the King and all our company
else being drowned, we will inherit here. Here, bear
my bottle, fellow Trinculo; we'll fill him by and by
again.

CALIBAN *sings drunkenly*
Farewell, master; farewell, farewell! 180

TRINCULO A howling monster; a drunken monster.

CALIBAN   No more dams I'll make for fish,
                Nor fetch in firing at requiring,
                Nor scrape trenchering, nor wash dish.
                'Ban, 'ban, Cacaliban
                Has a new master; get a new man!
  Freedom, high-day! high-day, freedom! freedom,
high-day, freedom!
STEPHANO O brave monster! lead the way.

                                    [*Exeunt*

ACT THREE, scene 1

Enter . . . log This opening provides a parallel and contrast with Caliban's appearance at the beginning of the previous scene 'with a burden of wood'. Prospero has set both to physical work, but their reactions, and the language in which they express them, are very different. The present scene may be imagined as taking place in front of Prospero's cell.

1–2	their . . . off *the trouble they cause is cancelled by the delight one takes in doing them. This is one of a whole series of antitheses through which Ferdinand's speech proceeds.*
5	as odious *as it is odious in itself*
6	which *whom*
	quickens *brings to life*
8	crabbed *bad-tempered*
11	Upon . . . injunction *In response to a severe command*
12–13	such . . . executor *such a menial task was never carried out by such a noble person*
13	I forget *I am forgetting the work I have to do*
15	Most . . . it *The sweet thoughts are busiest in my head when I am busiest at my work (?). The general sense is clear, but the exact meaning is uncertain; the Folio text reads* busie lest, *and various emendations have been proposed.*
19	weep *i.e. drip with resin, as logs sometimes do when being burnt*
20	safe *securely occupied*

ACT THREE

Scene 1. *Enter* FERDINAND, *bearing a log*

FERDINAND There be some sports are painful, and their
  labour
  Delight in them sets off; some kinds of baseness
  Are nobly undergone; and most poor matters
  Point to rich ends. This my mean task
  Would be as heavy to me as odious, but
  The mistress which I serve quickens what's
   dead,
  And makes my labours pleasures. O, she is
  Ten times more gentle than her father's crabbed;
  And he's composed of harshness. I must remove
  Some thousands of these logs, and pile them up, 10
  Upon a sore injunction; my sweet mistress
  Weeps when she sees me work, and says such
   baseness
  Had never like executor. I forget;
  But these sweet thoughts do even refresh my
   labours,
  Most busiest, when I do it.
Enter MIRANDA. *At the same time,* PROSPERO *enters on an*
   upper level, unseen by those below
MIRANDA   Alas, now pray you
  Work not so hard; I would the lightning had
  Burnt up those logs that thou'rt enjoined to pile;
  Pray set it down, and rest you. When this burns,
  'Twill weep for having wearied you. My father
  Is hard at study; pray now, rest yourself; 20
  He's safe for these three hours.
FERDINAND   O most dear mistress,
  The sun will set before I shall discharge
  What I must strive to do.
MIRANDA   If you'll sit down,
  I'll bear your logs the while. Pray give me that;
  I'll carry it to the pile.

31   infected *i.e. with love*

33–4   'tis ... night *when it is really night-time, if you are with me it seems like morning*

35   Chiefly that *Mainly in order that*

37   hest *command*
       Admired Miranda *Both words mean 'wonderful': Ferdinand is exclaiming at the suitability of her name to her nature.*

38   top of admiration *highest of wonders*

40   eyed ... regard *looked with great admiration at*

43–4   never ... soul *never have I loved any woman so completely*

45   owed *possessed*

46   put ... foil *defeated it*

52–3   How ... of *I am ignorant of what men may look like in other places*

54   dower *dowry*

FERDINAND   No, precious creature,
I had rather crack my sinews, break my back,
Than you should such dishonour undergo,
While I sit lazy by.

MIRANDA   It would become me
As well as it does you; and I should do it
With much more ease, for my good will is to it,   30
And yours it is against.

PROSPERO [*Aside*]   Poor worm, thou art infected;
This visitation shows it.

MIRANDA   You look wearily.

FERDINAND No, noble mistress, 'tis fresh morning with
  me
When you are by at night. I do beseech you –
Chiefly that I might set it in my prayers –
What is your name?

MIRANDA   Miranda – O my father,
I have broke your hest to say so!

FERDINAND   Admired Miranda,
Indeed the top of admiration, worth
What's dearest to the world! Full many a lady
I have eyed with best regard, and many a time   40
Th' harmony of their tongues hath into bondage
Brought my too diligent ear. For several virtues
Have I liked several women; never any
With so full soul, but some defect in her
Did quarrel with the noblest grace she owed,
And put it to the foil. But you, O you,
So perfect and so peerless, are created
Of every creature's best.

MIRANDA   I do not know
One of my sex; no woman's face remember,
Save from my glass mine own; nor have I seen   50
More that I may call men than you, good friend,
And my dear father. How features are abroad
I am skilless of; but, by my modesty,
The jewel in my dower, I would not wish

Any companion in the world but you;
Nor can imagination form a shape
Besides yourself to like of. But I prattle
Something too wildly, and my father's precepts
I therein do forget.

FERDINAND   I am in my condition
A prince, Miranda; I do think, a king –   60
I would not so! – and would no more endure
This wooden slavery than to suffer
The flesh-fly blow my mouth. Hear my soul
    speak:
The very instant that I saw you, did
My heart fly to your service, there resides
To make me slave to it, and for your sake
Am I this patient log-man.

MIRANDA   Do you love me?

FERDINAND O heaven, O earth, bear witness to this
    sound,
And crown what I profess with kind event
If I speak true; if hollowly, invert   70
What best is boded me, to mischief. I
Beyond all limit of what else i' the world,
Do love, prize, honour you.

MIRANDA   I am a fool
To weep at what I am glad of.

PROSPERO [Aside]   Fair encounter
Of two most rare affections. Heavens rain grace
On that which breeds between 'em.

FERDINAND   Wherefore weep you?

MIRANDA At mine unworthiness, that dare not offer
What I desire to give; and much less take
What I shall die to want. But this is trifling,
And all the more it seeks to hide itself   80
The bigger bulk it shows. Hence bashful
    cunning,
And prompt me plain and holy innocence.
I am your wife, if you will marry me;

If not, I'll die your maid. To be your fellow
You may deny me, but I'll be your servant
Whether you will or no.

FERDINAND   My mistress, dearest,
And I thus humble ever.

MIRANDA   My husband, then?

FERDINAND Ay, with a heart as willing
As bondage e'er of freedom. Here's my hand.

MIRANDA And mine, with my heart in't. And now
farewell   90
Till half an hour hence.

FERDINAND   A thousand thousand.

[*Exeunt* FERDINAND *and* MIRANDA, *in different directions*

PROSPERO So glad of this as they I cannot be,
Who are surprised with all, but my rejoicing
At nothing can be more. I'll to my book,
For yet ere supper-time must I perform
Much business appertaining.   [*Exit*

Scene 2. *Enter* CALIBAN, STEPHANO, *and* TRINCULO

STEPHANO Tell not me! When the butt is out we will
drink water, not a drop before. Therefore bear up,
and board 'em. Servant-monster, drink to me.

TRINCULO Servant-monster? The folly of this island!
They say there's but five upon this isle; we are three
of them; if th'other two be brained like us, the state
totters.

STEPHANO Drink, servant-monster, when I bid thee;
thy eyes are almost set in thy head.

TRINCULO Where should they be set else? He were a   10
brave monster indeed if they were set in his tail.

STEPHANO My man-monster hath drowned his tongue in
sack. For my part the sea cannot drown me; I swam,
ere I could recover the shore, five-and-thirty leagues
off and on. By this light, thou shalt be my lieutenant,
monster, or my standard.

17	no standard *incapable of standing*
18	run *run away*
19	go *walk*
	lie *Pun: both 'tell lies' and 'recline'.*

| 25–6 | in case . . . constable *in the frame of mind to elbow an officer of the law out of my way* |

| 33 | natural *idiot. (Trinculo is surprised because, in another sense, a monster is something unnatural.)* |

| 36 | the next tree! *i.e. the nearest tree shall be your gallows* |

| 51 | supplant *dislodge* |

TRINCULO Your lieutenant, if you list; he's no standard.

STEPHANO We'll not run, Monsieur Monster.

TRINCULO Nor go neither; but you'll lie like dogs, and yet say nothing neither. 20

STEPHANO Moon-calf, speak once in thy life, if thou beest a good moon-calf.

CALIBAN How does thy honour? Let me lick thy shoe; I'll not serve him, he is not valiant.

TRINCULO Thou liest, most ignorant monster; I am in case to jostle a constable. Why, thou debauched fish, thou, was there ever man a coward that hath drunk so much sack as I today? Wilt thou tell a monstrous lie, being but half a fish and half a monster?

CALIBAN Lo, how he mocks me; wilt thou let him, my 30 lord?

TRINCULO 'Lord,' quoth he? That a monster should be such a natural!

CALIBAN Lo, lo, again. Bite him to death, I prithee.

STEPHANO Trinculo, keep a good tongue in your head. If you prove a mutineer, the next tree! The poor monster's my subject, and he shall not suffer indignity.

CALIBAN I thank my noble lord. Wilt thou be pleased to hearken once again to the suit I made to thee? 40

STEPHANO Marry will I. Kneel and repeat it; I will stand, and so shall Trinculo.

Enter ARIEL, *invisible*

CALIBAN As I told thee before, I am subject to a tyrant, a sorcerer, that by his cunning hath cheated me of the island.

ARIEL Thou liest.

CALIBAN [*To* TRINCULO] 'Thou liest,' thou jesting monkey, thou?
    I would my valiant master would destroy thee.
    I do not lie.

STEPHANO Trinculo, if you trouble him any more in's 50 tale, by this hand, I will supplant some of your teeth.

TRINCULO Why, I said nothing.

STEPHANO Mum then, and no more. Proceed.

CALIBAN I say by sorcery he got this isle;
From me he got it. If thy Greatness will,
Revenge it on him, for I know thou dar'st,
But this thing dare not.

STEPHANO That's most certain.

CALIBAN Thou shalt be lord of it, and I'll serve thee.

STEPHANO How now shall this be compassed? Canst 60
bring me to the party?

CALIBAN Yea, yea, my lord, I'll yield him thee asleep,
Where thou mayst knock a nail into his head.

ARIEL Thou liest, thou canst not.

CALIBAN What a pied ninny's this? Thou scurvy
patch!
I do beseech thy Greatness, give him blows,
And take his bottle from him. When that's gone,
He shall drink naught but brine, for I'll not
show him
Where the quick freshes are.

STEPHANO Trinculo, run into no further danger. Inter- 70
rupt the monster one word further, and by this
hand, I'll turn my mercy out o' doors, and make a
stock-fish of thee.

TRINCULO Why, what did I? I did nothing. I'll go farther
off.

STEPHANO Didst thou not say he lied?

ARIEL Thou liest.

STEPHANO Did I so? Take thou that! [*Beats* TRINCULO]
As you like this, give me the lie another time.

TRINCULO I did not give the lie. Out o' your wits, and 80
hearing too? A pox o' your bottle, this can sack and
drinking do. A murrain on your monster, and the
devil take your fingers!

CALIBAN Ha, ha, ha!

STEPHANO [*To* CALIBAN] Now forward with your tale.
[*To* TRINCULO] Prithee stand further off.

92	paunch *stab in the stomach*
93	wezand *wind-pipe*
95	sot *fool*
97	Burn but *Only burn*
98	utensils *furnishings. Both* utensils *and* nonpareil (*line 102*) *are difficult words, and Shakespeare therefore emphasises that Caliban has got them from Prospero, and hints that he may not fully understand them.*
102–3	I . . . she *A reminder that, just as Miranda has never seen a second man, so Caliban has never seen a second woman.*
103	But only *Except for*
106	become *adorn*
107	brave brood *fine offspring*
109	save our Graces! *God save our Majesties!*

CALIBAN Beat him enough. After a little time
    I'll beat him too.
STEPHANO   Stand farther. [*To* CALIBAN]
                    Come, proceed.
CALIBAN Why, as I told thee, 'tis a custom with him
    I' th' afternoon to sleep. There thou mayst brain
        him,   90
    Having first seized his books; or with a log
    Batter his skull, or paunch him with a stake,
    Or cut his wezand with thy knife. Remember
    First to possess his books, for without them
    He's but a sot, as I am, nor hath not
    One spirit to command; they all do hate him
    As rootedly as I. Burn but his books.
    He has brave útensils (for so he calls them)
    Which, when he has a house, he'll deck withal.
    And that most deeply to consider is   100
    The beauty of his daughter. He himself
    Calls her a nonpareil; I never saw a woman
    But only Sycorax, my dam, and she;
    But she as far surpasseth Sycorax,
    As great'st does least.
STEPHANO   Is it so brave a lass?
CALIBAN Ay, lord, she will become thy bed, I warrant,
    And bring thee forth brave brood.
STEPHANO Monster, I will kill this man; his daughter
    and I will be King and Queen – save our Graces! –
    and Trinculo and thyself shall be viceroys. Dost thou 110
    like the plot, Trinculo?
TRINCULO Excellent.
STEPHANO Give me thy hand; I am sorry I beat thee;
    but while thou livest keep a good tongue in thy head.
CALIBAN Within this half hour will he be asleep;
    Wilt thou destroy him then?
STEPHANO   Ay, on mine honour.
ARIEL [*Aside*] This will I tell my master.
CALIBAN Thou mak'st me merry; I am full of pleasure;

119   troll the catch *sing the round-song*
120   but while-ere *only a little while ago*
121–2   any reason *anything reasonable*

123   cout *make a fool of*
124   scout *jeer at*

tabor *small drum*

130–1   in thy likeness *in your true shape*
131   take't . . . list *do what you like about it*

133   He . . . debts *A proverb. Sins are a kind of debt.*

138   airs *tunes*

139   twangling *An invented word, whose sound suggests its meaning.*

148   When . . . destroyed *Caliban is more sensible than the man he has made a god, and will not be distracted from the main purpose by dreams of what will follow. For Stephano, the plot to kill Prospero has already become only a 'story' (line 150).*

122

Let us be jocund. Will you troll the catch
You taught me but while-ere?   120

STEPHANO At thy request, monster, I will do reason, any
reason. Come on, Trinculo, let us sing.

He sings

Flout 'em and cout 'em
And scout 'em and flout 'em;
Thought is free.

CALIBAN That's not the tune.

ARIEL *plays the tune on a tabor and pipe*

STEPHANO What is this same?

TRINCULO This is the tune of our catch, played by the
picture of Nobody.

STEPHANO If thou beest a man, show thyself in thy 130
likeness. If thou beest a devil, take't as thou list.

TRINCULO O, forgive me my sins!

STEPHANO He that dies pays all debts. I defy thee.
Mercy upon us!

CALIBAN Art thou afeard?

STEPHANO No, monster, not I.

CALIBAN Be not afeard; the isle is full of noises,
Sounds and sweet airs, that give delight and
hurt not.
Sometimes a thousand twangling instruments
Will hum about mine ears; and sometimes voices, 140
That if I then had waked after long sleep,
Will make me sleep again; and then, in dream-
ing,
The clouds methought would open, and show
riches
Ready to drop upon me, that when I waked
I cried to dream again.

STEPHANO This will prove a brave kingdom to me,
where I shall have my music for nothing.

CALIBAN When Prospero is destroyed.

STEPHANO That shall be by and by: I remember the
story.   150

155   Wilt come? *Caliban wants to go off to Prospero's cell;
        Trinculo is urging him to follow the music instead, like
        Stephano.*

ACT THREE, scene 3

1   By'r lakin *By Our Lady (the Virgin Mary).*

3   forth-rights and meanders *straight and twisting paths*

5   attached *seized*

7–8   keep . . . flatterer *no longer allow it to deceive me.*

10   frustrate *vain*

13   effect *carry out*
13–14   The next . . . throughly *We will make thorough use of
        the next opportunity (to kill Alonso)*

        on the top *above*

        banquet *light refreshments (e.g. fruit and wine)*
        gentle . . . salutations *gracious miming of greetings*

124

TRINCULO The sound is going away; let's follow it, and after do our work.

STEPHANO Lead, monster, we'll follow. I would I could see this taborer, he lays it on.

TRINCULO Wilt come? I'll follow Stephano.   [*Exeunt*

Scene 3. *Enter* ALONSO, SEBASTIAN, ANTHONIO, GONZALO, ADRIAN, FRANCISCO, *and other* COURTIERS

GONZALO By'r lakin, I can go no further, sir;
  My old bones aches. Here's a maze trod indeed
  Through forth-rights and meanders; by your
   patience,
  I needs must rest me.

ALONSO   Old lord, I cannot blame thee,
  Who am myself attached with weariness
  To the dulling of my spirits. Sit down and rest.
  Even here will I put off my hope, and keep it
  No longer for my flatterer: he is drowned
  Whom thus we stray to find, and the sea mocks
  Our frustrate search on land. Well, let him go. 10

ANTHONIO [*Aside to* SEBASTIAN] I am right glad that he's
  so out of hope.
  Do not for one repulse forego the purpose
  That you resolved t'effect.

SEBASTIAN [*Aside to* ANTHONIO] The next advantage
  Will we take throughly.

ANTHONIO [*Aside to* SEBASTIAN] Let it be tonight,
  For, now they are oppressed with travel, they
  Will not nor cannot use such vigilance
  As when they are fresh.

SEBASTIAN [*Aside to* ANTHONIO] I say tonight. No more.
Solemn and strange music; and PROSPERO *on the top,
invisible. Enter several strange shapes, bringing in a
banquet, and dance about it with gentle actions of saluta-
tions; and, inviting the King, etc., to eat, they depart*

ALONSO   What harmony is this? My good friends,
         hark!
GONZALO   Marvellous sweet music!
ALONSO   Give us kind keepers, heavens! What were
         these?   20
SEBASTIAN   A living drollery. Now I will believe
         That there are unicorns; that in Arabia
         There is one tree, the phoenix' throne, one
            phoenix
         At this hour reigning there.
ANTHONIO   I'll believe both;
         And what does else want credit, come to me
         And I'll be sworn 'tis true. Travellers ne'er
            did lie,
         Though fools at home condemn 'em.
GONZALO   If in Naples
         I should report this now, would they believe
            me?
         If I should say I saw such islanders –
         For certes these are people of the island –   30
         Who though they are of monstrous shape, yet
            note
         Their manners are more gentle, kind, than of
         Our human generation you shall find
         Many, nay almost any.
PROSPERO [*Aside*]   Honest lord,
         Thou hast said well: for some of you there
            present
         Are worse than devils.
ALONSO   I cannot too much muse
         Such shapes, such gesture, and such sound,
            expressing –
         Although they want the use of tongue – a kind
         Of excellent dumb discourse.
PROSPERO [*Aside*]   Praise in departing.
FRANCISCO   They vanished strangely.
SEBASTIAN   No matter, since   40

41	viands *food*
43–6	When . . . breasts *More favourite travellers' tales of Shakespeare's age.*
44–5	mountaineers/Dew-lapped *mountain-dwellers with hanging folds of skin on their necks*
48	putter-out . . . one *traveller who deposits a sum of money with an insurer, to be repaid fivefold if he returns safely. This was a common device in Shakespeare's time, so the phrase means 'ordinary traveller'.*
48–9	will . . . warrant *will guarantee the truth*
50	Although . . . matter *Although it should be my last meal, it does not matter*
	harpy *monster with woman's face and body and bird's wings and claws, which was supposed to act as an instrument of divine vengeance*
	quaint device *ingenious stage-trick (the food could be removed from a trapdoor in the table while it was covered with the harpy's wings)*
54	hath to instrument *has under its control*
55–6	the never-surfeited . . . you *has caused the sea, which can never have too much to eat, to belch up. (Normally the sea digests all it swallows; it takes a special intervention of Destiny to make it belch up these three.)*
59	even . . . valour *with that very kind of courage that makes (i.e. the false courage caused by madness)*
61	ministers of Fate *those who carry out Fate's decrees*
	elements *materials*
62	Of whom . . . tempered *Of which your swords are composed*
64	still-closing *always closing themselves again after being stabbed*
64–5	diminish . . . plume *lessen my plumage by the tiniest feather*

128

They have left their viands behind, for we have
   stomachs.
Will't please you taste of what is here?

ALONSO   Not I.

GONZALO Faith sir, you need not fear. When we were
   boys
Who would believe that there were mountaineers
Dew-lapped like bulls, whose throats had
   hanging at 'em
Wallets of flesh? Or that there were such men
Whose heads stood in their breasts? which now
   we find
Each putter-out of five for one will bring us
Good warrant of.

ALONSO   I will stand to, and feed;
Although my last, no matter, since I feel   50
The best is past. Brother, my lord the Duke,
Stand to, and do as we.

Thunder and lightning. Enter ARIEL *like a harpy, claps
his wings upon the table, and with a quaint device the
banquet vanishes*

ARIEL You are three men of sin, whom Destiny,
That hath to instrument this lower world
And what is in't, the never-surfeited sea
Hath caused to belch up you; and on this island,
Where man doth not inhabit, you 'mongst men
Being most unfit to live, I have made you mad;
And even with such-like valour men hang and
   drown
Their proper selves.

           They draw their swords

                 You fools, I and my fellows   60
Are ministers of Fate; the elements
Of whom your swords are tempered may as well
Wound the loud winds, or with bemocked-at
   stabs
Kill the still-closing waters, as diminish

66   like *similarly*

71   requit it *given you your reward for the deed*

73   The Powers *A deliberately vague way of referring to*
            whatever are the ultimate powers in the world of the
            play – Fate, Destiny, God, the gods.

76   pronounce by me *announce through me that*
77–8   any . . . once *any instantaneous death could be*

79   whose wraths . . . from *and the means to protect your-*
            self from the Powers' wrath

80   else falls *will otherwise fall*

82   clear *blameless*

            mocks and mows *mocking gestures and grimaces*

83–4   Bravely . . . devouring *You have acted the part of this*
            harpy admirably, my Ariel; your performance had a
            ravishing grace

85   bated *left out*
86–7   good . . . strange *admirable realism and unusual*
            attentiveness
87–8   meaner . . . done *subordinate agents have acted the parts*
            appropriate to their natures
88   high charms *great spells*
89   knit up *entangled*

One dowle that's in my plume. My fellow-
    ministers
Are like invulnerable; if you could hurt,
Your swords are now too massy for your
    strengths,
And will not be uplifted. But remember –
For that's my business to you – that you three
From Milan did supplant good Prospero,   70
Exposed unto the sea, which hath requit it,
Him, and his innocent child; for which foul deed,
The Powers, delaying, not forgetting, have
Incensed the seas and shores, yea, all the
    creatures
Against your peace. Thee of thy son, Alonso,
They have bereft, and do pronounce by me
Lingering perdition, worse than any death
Can be at once, shall step by step attend
You and your ways; whose wraths to guard you
    from –
Which here, in this most desolate isle, else falls   80
Upon your heads – is nothing but heart's sorrow,
And a clear life ensuing.

*He vanishes in thunder; then, to soft music, enter the
shapes again, and dance, with mocks and mows, and
carrying out the table*

PROSPERO Bravely the figure of this harpy hast thou
    Performed, my Ariel; a grace it had devouring.
    Of my instruction hast thou nothing bated
    In what thou hadst to say; so, with good life
    And observation strange, my meaner ministers
    Their several kinds have done. My high charms
        work,
    And these mine enemies are all knit up
    In their distractions: they now are in my power;   90
    And in these fits I leave them, while I visit
    Young Ferdinand, whom they suppose is
        drowned,

94–5	why . . . strange stare *Gonzalo, being innocent of the crime against Prospero, has not heard Ariel's denunciation.*
99	it did . . . trespass *the name 'Prospero', sung by the thunder, supplied a ground-bass to the music of the waves and winds as they sang of my sin*
100	Therefore . . . bedded *That is why my son is buried in the mud on the sea-bottom*
101	deeper . . . sounded *both words that continue the image of music, as well as referring to taking the depth of the water.*
	plummet *weight used for measuring the depth of the water*
102–3	But . . . o'er *If the devils will only come one at a time, I'll fight whole armies of them to the end*
103	second *supporter*
104	All three . . . desperate *The three react differently, however, in a way which anticipates the play's outcome. Alonso acknowledges his guilt and is plunged into despair, whereas Sebastian and Anthonio become frenziedly defiant.*
105	work *take effect*
108	ecstasy *madness*

And his and mine loved darling.   [*Exit*

GONZALO I'the name of something holy, sir, why stand
            you
            In this strange stare?

ALONSO   O, it is monstrous, monstrous!
            Methought the billows spoke, and told me of it;
            The winds did sing it to me; and the thunder,
            That deep and dreadful organ-pipe, pronounced
            The name of Prosper: it did bass my trespass.
            Therefore my son i'th' ooze is bedded; and   100
            I'll seek him deeper than e'er plummet sounded,
            And with him there lie mudded.   [*Exit*

SEBASTIAN   But one fiend at a time,
            I'll fight their legions o'er.

ANTHONIO   .I'll be thy second.
                        [*Exeunt* ANTHONIO *and* SEBASTIAN

GONZALO All three of them are desperate. Their great
            guilt,
            Like poison given to work a great time after,
            Now 'gins to bite the spirits. I do beseech you
            That are of suppler joints, follow them swiftly
            And hinder them from what this ecstasy
            May now provoke them to.

ADRIAN   Follow, I pray you.
                                    [*Exeunt*

ACT FOUR, scene 1

The scene can once again be imagined as in front of Prospero's cell.

3	third *third part*
4	who *whom*
7	strangely *wonderfully well*
8	ratify *formally confirm*
9	boast her off *make a boast of her*
11	halt *limp*
12	Against an oracle *Even though an oracle had declared otherwise*
14	purchased *won by your pains*
16	sanctimonious *holy (not with the modern suggestion of hypocrisy)*
18	aspersion *sprinkling (of divine grace)*
19	contract grow *betrothal fruitful*
19–20	Hate . . . Disdain . . . Discord *With these personifications performing symbolic actions, we seem already to have half-entered the world of the masque which is to follow. Hymen too is a common masque character.*
21	weeds *As opposed to the flowers with which the marriage-bed was usually decorated.*
23	As . . . you *As you hope Hymen's torches will burn with a clear flame at your wedding. (Hymen, the Roman god of marriage, was pictured carrying a burning torch. If it burned smokily, it was thought that the marriage would be unhappy.)*
24	issue *offspring*
25	such . . . now *love continuing as perfect as it is now*
	murkiest den *A suitable place for illicit love.*
26–7	strong'st . . . can *strongest temptation one's bad angel could offer. (It was often thought that each human being was accompanied by two angels such as Doctor Faustus has in Marlowe's play, one good, one bad.)*
28–9	to take . . . edge *so as to blunt the keen enjoyment*
29	that day *i.e. the day of his marriage to Miranda*

ACT FOUR

Scene 1. Enter PROSPERO, FERDINAND, *and* MIRANDA

PROSPERO If I have too austerely punished you,
      Your compensation makes amends, for I
      Have given you here a third of mine own life,
      Or that for which I live; who once again
      I tender to thy hand. All thy vexations
      Were but my trials of thy love, and thou
      Hast strangely stood the test. Here, afore
         heaven,
      I ratify this my rich gift. O Ferdinand,
      Do not smile at me that I boast her off,
      For thou shalt find she will outstrip all praise   10
      And make it halt behind her.
FERDINAND   I do believe it
      Against an oracle.
PROSPERO Then, as my gift and thine own acquisition,
      Worthily purchased, take my daughter. But
      If thou dost break her virgin-knot before
      All sanctimonious ceremonies may
      With full and holy rite be ministered,
      No sweet aspersion shall the heavens let fall
      To make this contract grow; but barren Hate,
      Sour-eyed Disdain and Discord shall bestrew   20
      The union of your bed with weeds so loathly
      That you shall hate it both: therefore take heed,
      As Hymen's lamps shall light you.
FERDINAND   As I hope
      For quiet days, fair issue, and long life,
      With such love as 'tis now, the murkiest den,
      The most oppòrtune place, the strong'st
         suggestion
      Our worser genius can, shall never melt
      Mine honour into lust, to take away
      The edge of that day's celebration

30–1   or Phoebus' . . . below *either the sun's horses are lamed or night is being forcibly kept below the horizon (i.e. the sun will never set and night will never come. Phoebus was the classical sun-god, who was carried daily across the sky in a chariot drawn by horses.)*

35   meaner fellows *inferior comrades*

37   rabble *crowd of spirits*

39   Incite . . . motion *Urge them to come quickly*

41   vanity *trifle. Prospero is speaking modestly, of course, but in another sense the masque does prove to be a vanity – an emptiness, a 'baseless fabric' which can be made to vanish into thin air.*

42   Presently? *At once?*

43   with a twink *before you can blink*

47   mop and mow *gestures and grimaces*

50   conceive *understand*

51–3   do . . . blood *do not be too much carried away by your love-making; solemn promises are easily broken when your feelings are aroused. (Presumably Prospero has turned round from speaking to Ariel, to find that the lovers have been embracing.)*

54–5   The . . . liver *My powers of self-control check the ardour of my passion. (The liver was thought to be the source of sexual passion.)*

56–7   bring . . . spirit *brings an excess of spirits, rather than have one too few*

When I shall think, or Phoebus' steeds are
    foundered, 30
Or Night kept chained below.

PROSPERO   Fairly spoke.
Sit then, and talk with her; she is thine own.
What, Ariel! my industrious servant, Ariel!

Enter ARIEL

ARIEL What would my potent master? Here I am.

PROSPERO Thou and thy meaner fellows your last
    service
Did worthily perform, and I must use you
In such another trick. Go bring the rabble,
O'er whom I give thee power, here, to this place.
Incite them to quick motion, for I must
Bestow upon the eyes of this young couple 40
Some vanity of mine Art: it is my promise,
And they expect it from me.

ARIEL   Presently?

PROSPERO Ay; with a twink.

ARIEL Before you can say 'come' and 'go,'
And breathe twice and cry 'so, so,'
Each one, tripping on his toe,
Will be here with mop and mow.
Do you love me, master? No?

PROSPERO Dearly, my delicate Ariel. Do not approach
Till thou dost hear me call.

ARIEL   Well; I conceive. [*Exit* 50

PROSPERO Look thou be true; do not give dalliance
Too much the rein; the strongest oaths are straw
To the fire i' the blood; be more abstemious,
Or else, good night your vow!

FERDINAND   I warrant you, sir,
The white cold virgin snow upon my heart
Abates the ardour of my liver.

PROSPERO   Well.
Now come, my Ariel, bring a corollary,

58	pertly *smartly*
	Iris *The goddess of the rainbow, and messenger to Juno, the queen of the Roman gods.*
60	Ceres *The goddess of the corn-bearing earth and of agriculture.*
	leas *meadows*
61	vetches *plants used for feeding animals*
63	thatched . . . keep *covered with the grass used for feeding them in the winter*
64	pionèd and twillèd *dug and woven (i.e. given a woven appearance by the action of the current and the weather; or by the use of woven twigs to support the bank) (?)*
65	spongy . . . betrims *damp April decorates (with flowers and leaves) at your command*
66	nymphs *Spirits supposed to inhabit different parts of the countryside; here probably the* Naiads *mentioned in line 128, nymphs of the streams, whose crowns are thought of as being the flowers and leaves on their banks.*
67	dismissèd *jilted*
68	lass-lorn *without a girl-friend*
	poll-clipt *pruned*
69	marge *shore*
70	thou . . . air *you enjoy the fresh air*
	Queen . . . sky *i.e. Juno*
71	watery arch *the rainbow*
72–4	with . . . sport *come and enjoy yourself here . . . with her Majesty*
74	peacocks *The birds, sacred to Juno, which drew her chariot through the sky.*
	amain *swiftly*
77	wife of Jupiter *i.e. Juno*
78	saffron *yellow*
81	bosky *covered with shrubs (opposite to* unshrubbed*)*
82	scarf *The rainbow is seen as a decoration adorning the earth.*
85	estate *bestow*
86–91	Tell . . . forsworn *This anxiety of Ceres (i.e. fruitfulness) to avoid Venus and Cupid (i.e. illicit love) is the symbolic equivalent of Prospero's warning in lines 14–23 that, unless Ferdinand and Miranda remain chaste until they are married, their marriage will produce only 'weeds'.*
87	her son *Cupid, the god of love*

Rather than want a spirit; appear, and pertly.

Soft music

No tongue; all eyes; be silent.

Enter IRIS

IRIS   *Ceres, most bounteous lady, thy rich leas*   60
Of wheat, rye, barley, vetches, oats and pease;
Thy turfy mountains, where live nibbling sheep,
And flat meads thatched with stover, them to keep;
Thy banks with pionèd and twillèd brims,
Which spongy April at thy hest betrims,
To make cold nymphs chaste crowns; and thy
     broom-groves,
Whose shadow the dismissèd bachelor loves,
Being lass-lorn; thy poll-clipt vineyard,
And thy sea-marge, sterile and rocky-hard,
Where thou thyself dost air – the Queen o' the
     sky,   70
Whose watery arch and messenger am I,
Bids thee leave these, and with her Sovereign
     Grace,
Here on this grass-plot, in this very place,
To come and sport. Her peacocks fly amain:
Approach, rich Ceres, her to entertain.

Enter CERES

CERES   *Hail, many-coloured messenger, that ne'er*
Dost disobey the wife of Jupiter;
Who, with thy saffron wings, upon my flowers
Diffusest honey-drops, refreshing showers,
And with each end of thy blue bow dost crown   80
My bosky acres and my unshrubbed down,
Rich scarf to my proud earth; why hath thy Queen
Summoned me hither, to this short-grassed green?

IRIS   *A contract of true love to celebrate,*
And some donation freely to estate
On the blest lovers.

CERES   *Tell me, heavenly bow,*
If Venus or her son, as thou dost know,

89	The . . . got *Pluto or Dis, the god of the dark underworld, fell in love with Proserpine, Ceres' daughter, and carried her off to his kingdom.*
90	blind boy *i.e. Cupid*
	scandalled *scandalous (because Cupid had caused so many scandals by making people fall in love with each other)*
91	forsworn *sworn to avoid*
92	her Deity *her (as one says of a Queen 'her Majesty')*
93	Cutting *Cutting through*
	Paphos *A city in Cyprus sacred to Venus.*
94	Dove-drawn *Venus's chariot was drawn by doves.*
	thought . . . done *they intended to perform*
96–7	no . . . lighted *they shall not go to bed together until they are married*
97	in vain *Referring to the intention of Venus and Cupid.*
98	Mars's . . . minion *Mars's lustful mistress (i.e. Venus, who was Mars's mistress although she was married to Vulcan)*
99	waspish-headed *irritable and ready to sting (with his arrows of love)*
100	sparrows *These, like doves, were associated with Venus.*
101	boy . . . out *ordinary boy*
101–2	Highest . . . comes *Juno, the highest Queen of state, is coming*
103	How does *How are you*
105	issue *offspring*
107–8	Long . . . you! *Long life and prosperity, and may you for ever enjoy new delights every hour!*
110	foison plenty *plentiful abundance*
111	garners *granaries*
113	with . . . bowing *bowed with the weight of their good fruit*
115	In . . . harvest *The moment harvest is over (thus there would be no winter)*

> *Do now attend the Queen? Since they did plot*
> *The means that dusky Dis my daughter got,*
> *Her and her blind boy's scandalled company*   90
> *I have forsworn.*

IRIS   *Of her society*
> *Be not afraid: I met her Deity*
> *Cutting the clouds towards Paphos, and her son*
> *Dove-drawn with her. Here thought they to have done*
> *Some wanton charm upon this man and maid,*
> *Whose vows are that no bed-right shall be paid*
> *Till Hymen's torch be lighted; but in vain;*
> *Mars's hot minion is returned again;*
> *Her waspish-headed son has broke his arrows,*
> *Swears he will shoot no more, but play with sparrows,*   100
> *And be a boy right out.*

CERES   *Highest Queen of state,*
> *Great Juno comes; I know her by her gait.*

Enter JUNO

JUNO *How does my bounteous sister? Go with me*
> *To bless this twain, that they may prosperous be*
> *And honoured in their issue.*

JUNO and CERES sing

JUNO *Honour, riches, marriage-blessing,*
> *Long continuance and increasing,*
> *Hourly joys be still upon you!*
> *Juno sings her blessings on you.*

CERES *Earth's increase, foison plenty,*   110
> *Barns and garners never empty;*
> *Vines with clustering bunches growing,*
> *Plants with goodly burden bowing;*
> *Spring come to you at the farthest*
> *In the very end of harvest.*
> *Scarcity and want shall shun you,*
> *Ceres' blessing so is on you.*

119   charmingly *magically*

123   wondered *Both 'wonder-working' and 'wonderful'.*

128   windring *winding and wandering (an invented word)*
129   sedged *woven from sedge (a plant which grows in wet places)*
130   crisp *rippling*

132   temperate *self-restrained*
133   contract *betrothal*

134   sicklemen *reapers*

138   footing *dance*
          properly habited *dressed suitably to their parts*

          heavily *sorrowfully*

142   avoid *go away*

142

FERDINAND This is a most majestic vision, and
          Harmonious charmingly. May I be bold
          To think these spirits?
PROSPERO   Spirits, which by mine Art 120
          I have from their confines called to enact
          My present fancies.
FERDINAND   Let me live here ever;
          So rare a wondered father and a wise
          Makes this place Paradise.

    JUNO *and* CERES *whisper, and send* IRIS *on employment*

PROSPERO   Sweet now, silence!
          Juno and Ceres whisper seriously;
          There's something else to do; hush, and be mute,
          Or else our spell is marred.
IRIS *You nymphs, called Naiads, of the windring brooks,*
          With your sedged crowns, and ever-harmless looks,
          Leave your crisp channels, and on this green
              land   130
          Answer your summons; Juno does command.
          Come, temperate nymphs, and help to celebrate
          A contract of true love; be not too late.

                    Enter certain NYMPHS

          You sun-burned sicklemen, of August weary,
          Come hither from the furrow, and be merry,
          Make holiday; your rye-straw hats put on,
          And these fresh nymphs encounter every one
          In country footing.

Enter certain REAPERS, *properly habited; they join with*
the NYMPHS *in a graceful dance, towards the end where-*
of PROSPERO *starts suddenly and speaks, after which,*
to a strange, hollow and confused noise, they heavily
                    vanish

PROSPERO [*Aside*] I had forgot that foul conspiracy
          Of the beast Caliban and his confederates   140
          Against my life: the minute of their plot
          Is almost come. [*To the* SPIRITS] Well done!
          avoid; no more.

144   works *agitates*

145   distempered *violent*
146   moved sort *troubled state of mind*

149   foretold you *told you before*

153   globe *i.e. of the earth; but perhaps with an allusion to the famous theatre in London.*
154   all . . . inherit *all things that inhabit it*
156   rack *thin cloud*
157   on *of*
158   rounded *rounded off (or perhaps 'crowned')*

164   with a thought *as quick as my thought of you*
         thank thee *i.e. for organising the masque*
165   Thy . . . to *I follow closely upon your thoughts (in two senses: being instantaneously aware of them and obeying them).*
167   presented Ceres *An ambiguous phrase: it could mean that Ariel played the part of Ceres in the masque; or, more probably, that he played the part of Iris and thus presented (i.e. introduced) Ceres; or possibly that he presented the masque of Ceres only in the sense that he stage-managed it.*
170   Say again *We have to suppose that Ariel and Prospero have previously discussed this off-stage.*

144

FERDINAND This is strange: your father's in some passion
That works him strongly.

MIRANDA   Never till this day
Saw I him touched with anger so distempered.

PROSPERO You do look, my son, in a moved sort,
As if you were dismayed: be cheerful, sir.
Our revels now are ended; these our actors,
As I foretold you, were all spirits, and
Are melted into air, into thin air.   150
And, like the baseless fabric of this vision,
The cloud-capped towers, the gorgeous palaces,
The solemn temples, the great globe itself,
Yea, all which it inherit, shall dissolve,
And, like this insubstantial pageant faded,
Leave not a rack behind. We are such stuff
As dreams are made on; and our little life
Is rounded with a sleep. Sir, I am vexed;
Bear with my weakness, my old brain is troub-
led;
Be not disturbed with my infirmity.   160
If you be pleased, retire into my cell,
And there repose; a turn or two I'll walk,
To still my beating mind.

FERDINAND *and* MIRANDA   We wish your peace.
                                        [*Exeunt*

PROSPERO [*To* ARIEL, *who is off-stage*] Come with a
thought! I thank thee, Ariel; come.
                    Enter ARIEL

ARIEL Thy thoughts I cleave to. What's thy pleasure?

PROSPERO   Spirit,
We must prepare to meet with Caliban.

ARIEL Ay, my commander, when I presented Ceres
I thought to have told thee of it, but I feared
Lest I might anger thee.

PROSPERO Say again, where didst thou leave these
varlets?   170

172	smote *struck at*
174–5	bending . . . project *moving gradually towards their goal of killing Prospero*
176	unbacked *not broken in*
177	Advanced *Raised*
178–9	charmed . . . That *cast a spell on their hearing so that*
180	Toothed *Prickly*
	goss *gorse*
181	entered *pierced*
182	filthy-mantled *covered with scum*
183	that *so that*
184	O'erstunk *Outstank (i.e. the lake, through being stirred up by them, smelt even worse than their feet).*
186	trumpery *worthless things (referring to the 'glistering apparel' of the next stage direction)*
187	stale *bait*
189	Nurture *Education, civilisation (see Introduction, p. 6)*
	pains *trouble*
192	cankers *grows more corrupt*
	plague *torment*
193	Even to roaring *Until they roar aloud with pain*
	line *lime-tree (a tree would be a common stage property)*
	Enter . . . wet *From this point to the end of the scene Prospero and Ariel are unseen by the others, either by taking on invisibility or by hiding.*
194–5	that . . . fall *Moles were supposed to have especially keen hearing. Though Caliban's nature may be untouched by nurture, poetry such as this, at once earthy and delicate, shows that it is less vulgar than the civilised natures of his accomplices.*
196	fairy *i.e. Ariel*
197–8	played . . . us *made fools of us by leading us like a Jack o' lantern or will-o'-the-wisp*

ARIEL I told you, sir, they were red-hot with drinking,
So full of valour that they smote the air
For breathing in their faces; beat the ground
For kissing of their feet; yet always bending
Towards their project. Then I beat my tabor,
At which like unbacked colts they pricked their
ears,
Advanced their eyelids, lifted up their noses
As they smelt music; so I charmed their ears
That, calf-like, they my lowing followed through
Toothed briers, sharp furzes, pricking goss and
thorns,   180
Which entered their frail shins; at last I left them
I' the filthy-mantled pool beyond your cell,
There dancing up to the chins, that the foul
lake
O'erstunk their feet.
PROSPERO   This was well done, my bird.
Thy shape invisible retain thou still;
The trumpery in my house, go bring it hither,
For stale to catch these thieves.
ARIEL   I go, I go. [Exit
PROSPERO A devil, a born devil, on whose nature
Nurture can never stick; on whom my pains,
Humanely taken, all, all lost, quite lost;   190
And as with age his body uglier grows,
So his mind cankers. I will plague them all,
Even to roaring.
        Enter ARIEL, *loaden with glistering apparel, etc.*
                        Come, hang them on this line.
        Enter CALIBAN, STEPHANO *and* TRINCULO, *all wet*
CALIBAN   Pray you tread softly, that the blind mole
may not
Hear a foot fall; we now are near his cell.
STEPHANO Monster, your fairy, which you say is a
harmless fairy, has done little better than played the
jack with us.

207	hoodwink . . . mischance *put this misfortune out of mind. (The allusion is to the hood put over a hunting hawk's head to make it harmless.)*
210	disgrace . . . dishonour *As if their bottles were like regimental colours, which it would be a dishonour to lose.*
214	fetch off *recapture*
214–15	o'er ears *covered up to the ears in water*
218	good mischief *good wickedness (a self-contradiction)*
220	aye *ever*
223–4	O . . . Stephano *There was an old ballad with the lines*

> King Stephen was a worthy peer,
> His breeches cost him but a crown

which is alluded to here.

226–7	we . . . frippery *we are good judges of cast-offs*
227	frippery *old clothes shop*
228	Put off *Take off*

TRINCULO   Monster, I do smell all horse-piss, at which
my nose is in great indignation.   200
STEPHANO   So is mine. Do you hear, monster? If
I should take a displeasure against you, look
you, –
TRINCULO   Thou wert but a lost monster.
CALIBAN   Good my lord, give me thy favour still.
Be patient, for the prize I'll bring thee to
Shall hoodwink this mischance; therefore speak
     softly;
All's hushed as midnight yet.
TRINCULO   Ay, but to lose our bottles in the pool –
STEPHANO   There is not only disgrace and dishonour in   210
that, monster, but an infinite loss.
TRINCULO   That's more to me than my wetting; yet
this is your harmless fairy, monster.
STEPHANO   I will fetch off my bottle, though I be o'er
ears for my labour.
CALIBAN   Prithee, my King, be quiet. Seest thou
     here,
This is the mouth o' the cell: no noise, and enter.
Do that good mischief which may make this
     island
Thine own for ever, and I, thy Caliban,
For aye thy foot-licker.   220
STEPHANO   Give me thy hand; I do begin to have
bloody thoughts.
TRINCULO   O King Stephano, O peer, O worthy
Stephano, look what a wardrobe here is for thee!
CALIBAN   Let it alone, thou fool, it is but trash.
TRINCULO   O ho, monster! we know what belongs to a
frippery. O King Stephano!
STEPHANO   Put off that gown, Trinculo; by this hand,
I'll have that gown.
TRINCULO   Thy Grace shall have it.   230
CALIBAN   The dropsy drown this fool! What do you
     mean

luggage *useless encumbrances*
Let's alone *Let us go off without it*

crown *i.e. of the head*

237 jerkin *A kind of jacket.*
under the line *A pun: 'under the lime-tree' and 'under the equinoctial line (i.e. equator)'.*

238 lose . . . hair *Because people crossing the equator often caught fevers which made their hair fall out.*

239 bald *threadbare*

240 by . . . level *systematically (still punning on* line *meaning 'lime-tree')*

240–1 and't . . . Grace *if it please your Grace*

242 garment *Kings in Shakespeare's time often gave clothes in payment or reward to their retainers.*

245 pass of pate *thrust of wit (*pate *meaning 'head')*

246 lime *The foolish pun is prolonged still further: bird-lime is sticky, and thieves are said to have it on their fingers.*

248 on't *of it*

251 lay-to . . . fingers *set your fingers to work*

252 hogshead *large wine-barrel*

divers *various*

256–8 Mountain . . . Silver . . . Fury . . . Tyrant *These are the names of the hounds (really spirits) which Prospero and Ariel, like huntsmen, are urging to chase the villains.*

260 charge *order*

261 dry *coming from the dryness of old age*

150

To dote thus on such luggage? Let's alone
And do the murder first: if he awake,
From toe to crown he'll fill our skins with
    pinches,
Make us strange stuff.

STEPHANO Be you quiet, monster. Mistress line, is not
this my jerkin? Now is the jerkin under the line;
now, jerkin, you are like to lose your hair, and prove
a bald jerkin.

TRINCULO Do, do; we steal by line and level, and't 240
like your Grace.

STEPHANO I thank thee for that jest; here's a garment
for't; wit shall not go unrewarded while I am King
of this country. 'Steal by line and level' is an excellent
pass of pate; there's another garment for't.

TRINCULO Monster, come put some lime upon your
fingers, and away with the rest.

CALIBAN   I will have none on't: we shall lose our time,
And all be turned to barnacles, or to apes
With foreheads villainous low.   250

STEPHANO Monster, lay-to your fingers: help to bear
this away, where my hogshead of wine is, or I'll turn
you out of my kingdom: go to, carry this.

TRINCULO And this.

STEPHANO Ay, and this.

A noise of hunters heard. Enter divers SPIRITS *in shape
of dogs and hounds, hunting them about;* PROSPERO *and*
                 ARIEL *setting them on*

PROSPERO Hey, Mountain, hey!

ARIEL   Silver! there it goes, Silver.

PROSPERO Fury, Fury! there, Tyrant, there! hark,
hark!

                Exeunt CALIBAN, STEPHANO *and* TRINCULO,
                        pursued by the SPIRITS

Go, charge my goblins that they grind their
    joints   260
With dry convulsions, shorten up their sinews

263   pard ... mountain *panther or leopard*

264   soundly *thoroughly*

With agèd cramps, and more pinch-spotted make them
Than pard or cat o' mountain.

ARIEL   Hark, they roar.

PROSPERO   Let them be hunted soundly. At this hour
Lies at my mercy all mine enemies;
Shortly shall all my labours end, and thou
Shalt have the air at freedom; for a little
Follow, and do me service.

                                        [*Exeunt*

ACT FIVE, scene 1

Although Prospero has withdrawn in order to put on his magic robes, the setting and characters are the same as at the end of the last scene. This is something very unusual in a Shakespeare play. The stage may be empty for a moment between the acts, to indicate the passage of time; or it is possible that the hunting of Stephano, Trinculo and Caliban was enacted (perhaps in the form of a dance) on the cleared stage.

1	project *experiment (a term used in alchemy)*
	gather to a head *approach its culmination*
2	crack *fail (again suggesting the possible explosion of a vessel in an unsuccessful alchemical experiment)*
3	Goes . . . carriage *Bears his burden without stooping (because so little is now left to do)*
8	gave in charge *ordered*
10	line-grove . . . cell *grove of lime-trees which protects your cell from the weather*
11	your release *you release them*
12	distracted *mad (a stronger sense than nowadays)*
17	eaves of reeds *a roof thatched with reeds*
18	affections *feelings*
23–4	One . . . they *A man like them, and one who feels pain as sharply as they do*
24	kindlier *Both 'more sympathetically' and 'more naturally'.*
25	with . . . quick *I am deeply wounded by the cruel injuries they have done me*

ACT FIVE

Scene 1. *Enter* PROSPERO *in his magic robes, and* ARIEL

PROSPERO Now does my project gather to a head:
　　　　 My charms crack not, my spirits obey, and Time
　　　　 Goes upright with his carriage. How's the day?

ARIEL　 On the sixth hour, at which time, my lord,
　　　　 You said our work should cease.

PROSPERO 　　　　　　　　　　 I did say so,
　　　　 When first I raised the tempest. Say, my spirit,
　　　　 How fares the King and's followers?

ARIEL　　　　　　　　　　　　 Confined together
　　　　 In the same fashion as you gave in charge,
　　　　 Just as you left them; all prisoners, sir,
　　　　 In the line-grove which weather-fends your
　　　　　　cell;　　　　　　　　　　　　　　　　　10
　　　　 They cannot budge till your release. The King,
　　　　 His brother, and yours, abide all three dis-
　　　　　　tracted,
　　　　 And the remainder mourning over them,
　　　　 Brimful of sorrow and dismay; but chiefly
　　　　 Him that you termed, sir, 'the good old lord
　　　　　　Gonzalo,'
　　　　 His tears run down his beard like winter's drops
　　　　 From eaves of reeds. Your charm so strongly
　　　　　　works 'em
　　　　 That, if you now beheld them, your affections
　　　　 Would become tender.

PROSPERO 　　　　　　　　 Dost thou think so, spirit?

ARIEL　 Mine would, sir, were I human.

PROSPERO 　　　　　　　　　　 And mine shall.　20
　　　　 Hast thou, which art but air, a touch, a feeling
　　　　 Of their afflictions, and shall not myself,
　　　　 One of their kind, that relish all as sharply
　　　　 Passion as they, be kindlier moved than thou art?
　　　　 Though with their high wrongs I am struck to
　　　　　　the quick,

155

27	take part *take sides*

27–30	The rarer . . . further *It is nobler to act in accordance with Christian virtue than to take vengeance. The whole intention behind my plan requires not the least further harshness towards them, because they are repentant of the wrongs they have done*
33	elves *These are the English equivalent of the nymphs mentioned earlier.*
	standing *not flowing (by contrast with brooks)*
35	Neptune *i.e. the sea*
	fly *flee*
36	demi-puppets *doll-like creatures*
37	green . . . ringlets *'fairy rings' in the grass*
38	not bites *will not feed*
39–40	that . . . curfew *Because it announces that night is coming.*
41	masters *skilled spirits (?)*
43	azured *blue-coloured*
44	dread *dreadful*
45	fire *i.e. lightning*
	rifted *split*
	Jove's *The oak-tree was sacred to Jove (Jupiter, king of the gods).*
46	bolt *i.e. the thunderbolt, supposed to be hurled by Jupiter*
47	spurs *roots*
49	oped *opened*
51	abjure *formally abandon*
	required *asked for*
53–4	work . . . for *control the consciousness of those for whom I have caused this magic in the air (i.e. restore the senses of the royal party with music). There is a pun on air, which also means 'tune'.*
54–7	staff . . . book *The recognised instruments and symbols of the magician's power*
55	certain *a fixed number of*
56	plummet *lead weight for measuring the depth of water*
	sound *take soundings (i.e. measure depth); but deeper . . . sound also continues the suggestion of music*

156

Yet with my nobler reason 'gainst my fury
Do I take part. The rarer action is
In virtue than in vengeance. They being penitent,
The sole drift of my purpose doth extend
Not a frown further: go, release them, Ariel.   30
My charms I'll break, their senses I'll restore,
And they shall be themselves.

ARIEL   I'll fetch them, sir. [*Exit*
PROSPERO Ye elves of hills, brooks, standing lakes, and
          groves,
And ye that on the sands with printless foot
Do chase the ebbing Neptune, and do fly him
When he comes back; you demi-puppets that
By moonshine do the green sour ringlets make,
Whereof the ewe not bites; and you whose
          pastime
Is to make midnight mushrooms, that rejoice
To hear the solemn curfew, by whose aid   40
(Weak masters though ye be) I have bedimmed
The noontide sun, called forth the mutinous
          winds,
And 'twixt the green sea and the azured vault
Set roaring war; to the dread rattling thunder
Have I given fire, and rifted Jove's stout oak
With his own bolt; the strong-based promontory
Have I made shake, and by the spurs plucked up
The pine and cedar; graves at my command
Have waked their sleepers, oped, and let 'em
          forth
By my so potent Art. But this rough magic   50
I here abjure: and when I have required
Some heavenly music – which even now I do –
To work mine end upon their senses, that
This airy charm is for, I'll break my staff,
Bury it certain fathoms in the earth,
And deeper than did ever plummet sound
I'll drown my book.

frantic *frenzied*

in like manner *similarly expressing madness*

circle *The magic circle, which Prospero has been drawing during his preceding soliloquy.*

58	and *which is*
59	unsettled fancy *deranged mind. Music was thought a cure for madness in Shakespeare's time.*
60	boiled *over-agitated*
61	spell-stopped *rooted to the spot by magic. The verse too comes to an abrupt halt with this word.*
63–4	even . . . drops *full of sympathy at the very sight of yours, drop tears as they do*
64	apace *rapidly*
65	as *in the same way as*
66–8	their . . . reason *their senses, as they are restored to sanity, begin to blow away the smoke of ignorance that covered their reason, and make it clear again. (Drunkenness and madness were thought of as being literally produced by fumes rising into the brain.)*
69–70	sir . . . follow'st *servant to your master (i.e. Alonso)*
70–1	pay . . . Home *repay fully your gracious behaviour*
73	was . . . act *abetted you in the deed*
74	pinched *tormented*
	Flesh and blood *Perhaps an exclamation – 'This is what one's own flesh and blood can do to one!' – or perhaps simply linked with the next phrase – 'You, my brother, my own flesh and blood, who . . .'.*
75–6	entertained . . . nature *harboured ambition and turned aside pity and natural brotherly feeling*
79–82	Their . . . muddy *An elaborate metaphor, in which consciousness is thought of as a sea, which swells as its tide rises to fill up the shore of reason, left foul and muddy while the senses were lost. The metaphor is most appropriate to a sea-surrounded island.*

Solemn music. Here enters ARIEL *before; then* ALONSO
with a frantic gesture, attended by GONZALO; SEBASTIAN
and ANTHONIO *in like manner, attended by* ADRIAN *and*
FRANCISCO: *they all enter the circle which* PROSPERO *had
made, and there stand charmed; which* PROSPERO *observing,*
speaks

A solemn air, and the best comforter
To an unsettled fancy, cure thy brains,
Now useless, boiled within thy skull! There
    stand,   60
For you are spell-stopped.
Holy Gonzalo, honourable man,
Mine eyes, even sociable to the show of thine,
Fall fellowly drops. The charm dissolves apace,
And as the morning steals upon the night,
Melting the darkness, so their rising senses
Begin to chase the ignorant fumes that mantle
Their clearer reason. O good Gonzalo,
My true preserver, and a loyal sir
To him thou follow'st, I will pay thy graces   70
Home, both in word and deed. Most cruelly
Didst thou, Alonso, use me and my daughter;
Thy brother was a furtherer in the act;
Thou art pinched for't now, Sebastian. Flesh and
    blood,
You, brother mine, that entertained ambition,
Expelled remorse and nature, who, with
    Sebastian –
Whose inward pinches therefore are most
    strong –
Would here have killed your King; I do forgive
    thee,
Unnatural though thou art. Their understanding
Begins to swell, and the approaching tide   80
Will shortly fill the reasonable shore,
That now lies foul and muddy – not one of them
That yet looks on me, or would know me. Ariel,

159

160

Fetch me the hat and rapier in my cell;
I will discase me, and myself present
As I was sometime Milan. Quickly, spirit;
Thou shalt ere long be free.

> ARIEL *sings and helps to attire him*
> Where the bee sucks, there suck I;
> In a cowslip's bell I lie;
> There I couch when owls do cry;   90
> On the bat's back I do fly
> After summer merrily.
> Merrily, merrily, shall I live now,
> Under the blossom that hangs on the bough.

PROSPERO   Why, that's my dainty Ariel. I shall miss
thee,
But yet thou shalt have freedom; so, so, so.
To the King's ship, invisible as thou art;
There shalt thou find the mariners asleep
Under the hatches: the Master and the Boat-
swain
Being awake, enforce them to this place,   100
And presently, I prithee.

ARIEL   I drink the air before me, and return
Or ere your pulse twice beat.

           [*Exit*

GONZALO   All torment, trouble, wonder and amaze-
ment
Inhabits here: some heavenly power guide us
Out of this fearful country!

PROSPERO   Behold, Sir King,
The wrongèd Duke of Milan, Prospero!
For more assurance that a living prince
Does now speak to thee, I embrace thy body;
And to thee and thy company I bid   110
A hearty welcome.

ALONSO   Whe'er thou beest he or no,
Or some enchanted trifle to abuse me,
As late I have been, I not know; thy pulse

115–17   Th'affliction ... story *There has been an improvement in the sickness of my mind, which I fear imprisoned me in madness. If these things are really happening, they will demand a very strange explanation*

121   thine age *you, old as you are*
122   confined *limited*

123–4   taste ... subtleties *The image is of eating the elaborate devices of icing and pastry, somewhat like modern wedding cakes, which were served at banquets in Shakespeare's time, and were called* subtleties.
126   brace *pair*
       were ... minded *if I wished*

128   justify *prove*

129   Devil *A contemporary of Shakespeare's might well have thought that only by the help of the Devil could a man know what by natural means he could not know. But Prospero's* No *denies this: his is not black magic, but white.*
132   Thy ... them *your grossest fault, and indeed all your many gross faults*
       require *demand*
133   perforce *necessarily*

138   How ... is *How deeply the pain of remembering this wounds me*

162

Beats as of flesh and blood; and, since I saw
   thee,
Th'affliction of my mind amends, with which
I fear a madness held me. This must crave,
And if this be at all, a most strange story.
Thy Dukedom I resign, and do entreat
Thou pardon me my wrongs; but how should
   Prospero
Be living, and be here?

PROSPERO [*To* GONZALO]   First, noble friend,   120
Let me embrace thine age, whose honour cannot
Be measured or confined.

GONZALO   Whether this be,
Or be not, I'll not swear.

PROSPERO   You do yet taste
Some subtleties o' th' isle, that will not let you
Believe things certain. Welcome, my friends all.
[*To* SEBASTIAN *and* ANTHONIO] But you, my brace
   of lords, were I so minded,
I here could pluck his Highness' frown upon you
And justify you traitors. At this time
I will tell no tales.

SEBASTIAN   The Devil speaks in him.

PROSPERO   No.
For you, most wicked sir, whom to call brother 130
Would even infect my mouth, I do forgive
Thy rankest fault – all of them – and require
My Dukedom of thee, which perforce I know
Thou must restore.

ALONSO   If thou beest Prospero,
Give us particulars of thy preservation,
How thou hast met us here, who three hours
   since
Were wracked upon this shore? where I have
   lost –
How sharp the point of this remembrance is –
My dear son Ferdinand.

139	woe *sorry*
140–1	Patience ... cure *It is too severe for patience to be of any use in helping me to get over it*
142–4	her help ... content *the help of Patience, who, by her mercy, has granted me her powerful help in my similar loss, so that I have come to accept it*
144	You ... loss? *Have you suffered a similar loss?*
145–6	As ... loss *My loss is as great as yours, and as recent; and, to make this great loss endurable*
146	much weaker *Because a surviving daughter would be a natural source of comfort in a family bereavement.*
150	That ... were *In order that they might be*
154–6	At ... truth *Are so astonished at this meeting that their gaping mouths seem to swallow up their intelligence, and they can scarcely believe that their eyes are doing their duty of telling them the truth*
157–8	howsoe'er ... senses *however much these events may have disturbed your reason*
162	on't *of it*
163–4	chronicle ... breakfast *story that would take many days to tell, not one that could be told while we are having a snack*

164

PROSPERO   I am woe for't, sir.
ALONSO   Irreparable is the loss, and Patience   140
          Says it is past her cure.
PROSPERO   I rather think
          You have not sought her help, of whose soft
             grace
          For the like loss, I have her sovereign aid,
          And rest myself content.
ALONSO   You the like loss?
PROSPERO   As great to me, as late; and, supportable
          To make the dear loss, have I means much
             weaker
          Than you may call to comfort you; for I
          Have lost my daughter.
ALONSO   A daughter?
          O heavens, that they were living both in Naples,
          The King and Queen there! That they were,
             I wish   150
          Myself were mudded in that oozy bed
          Where my son lies. When did you lose your
             daughter?
PROSPERO In this last tempest. I perceive these lords
          At this encounter do so much admire
          That they devour their reason, and scarce think
          Their eyes do offices of truth, their words
          Are natural breath; but howsoe'er you have
          Been jostled from your senses, know for certain
          That I am Prospero, and that very Duke
          Which was thrust forth of Milan; who most
             strangely   160
          Upon this shore where you were wracked was
             landed,
          To be the lord on't. No more yet of this,
          For 'tis a chronicle of day by day,
          Not a relation for a breakfast, nor
          Befitting this first meeting. Welcome, sir;
          This cell's my court; here have I few attendants,

                                                        165

167   abroad *about the place*

169   requite *repay*

       discovers *reveals, presumably by pulling back a curtain in front of a recess. The first speeches of Miranda and Ferdinand are playful in tone and are addressed to each other; they do not notice that they are no longer alone.*

172   play me false *Both 'cheat me (at chess)' and 'deceive me (in love)'; Ferdinand understands, or pretends to understand, only the first sense.*

174–5   Yes . . . play *O yes, you would argue me out of twenty kingdoms, if they were at stake between us, and so skilfully that I would call your cheating fair play*

177   twice *Once by Ferdinand's death at sea; a second time if Alonso discovered that what he now took to be Ferdinand was only a hallucination – which would be as painful as if Ferdinand were to die again.*

180   compass . . . about *surround you*

186   Your . . . be *You cannot have known each other for more than*

187   severed *parted*

And subjects none abroad. Pray you, look in:
My Dukedom since you have given me again,
I will requite you with as good a thing,
At least bring forth a wonder, to content ye   170
As much as me my Dukedom.

Here PROSPERO *discovers* FERDINAND *and* MIRANDA
playing at chess

MIRANDA   Sweet lord, you play me false.

FERDINAND   No, my dearest love,
I would not for the world.

MIRANDA   Yes, for a score of kingdoms, you should
wrangle,
And I would call it fair play.

ALONSO   If this prove
A vision of the island, one dear son
Shall I twice lose.

SEBASTIAN   A most high miracle.

FERDINAND [*Having seen* ALONSO] Though the seas
threaten, they are merciful;
I have cursed them without cause.

Kneels before ALONSO

ALONSO   Now all the blessings
Of a glad father compass thee about!   180
Arise, and say how thou cam'st here.

MIRANDA   O wonder!
How many goodly creatures are there here!
How beauteous mankind is! O brave new world
That has such people in't.

PROSPERO   'Tis new to thee.

ALONSO   What is this maid, with whom thou wast at
play?
Your eld'st acquaintance cannot be three hours.
Is she the goddess that hath severed us,
And brought us thus together?

FERDINAND   Sir, she is mortal;
But by immortal Providence she's mine.
I chose her when I could not ask my father   190

167

193	Of . . . renown *of whose fame I have so often heard*
194–5	of . . . life *i.e. he has restored me to life when you thought me drowned. Or possibly Ferdinand may think of his acquaintance with Miranda as a second life he has received from Prospero.*
195	second father *i.e. father-in-law*
196	I am hers *I will be her father-in-law*

200	heaviness . . . gone *cause for sorrow now past*
200–1	I . . . this *I have been weeping inwardly (for joy), or I would have spoken before. (Gonzalo is so talkative that Shakespeare makes him apologise for this one occasion when he has no moralising comment to offer immediately.)*
203	chalked forth *marked out*

| 205 | Was . . . issue *Was the Duke of Milan expelled from his city in order that his descendants* |

| 208 | lasting pillars *an enduring monument* |

| 212–13 | all . . . own *we have all found ourselves, at a time when we had lost the knowledge of our true identities* |

| 214–15 | Let . . . joy *Let anyone who does not wish you joy be unhappy for ever* |
| | amazedly *in a dazed way* |

For his advice, nor thought I had one. She
Is daughter to this famous Duke of Milan,
Of whom so often I have heard renown,
But never saw before; of whom I have
Received a second life; and second father
This lady makes him to me.

ALONSO   I am hers.
But O, how oddly will it sound, that I
Must ask my child forgiveness!

PROSPERO   There, sir, stop.
Let us not burden our remembrances with
A heaviness that's gone.

GONZALO   I have inly wept,   200
Or should have spoke ere this. Look down, you
    gods,
And on this couple drop a blessèd crown;
For it is you that have chalked forth the way
Which brought us hither.

ALONSO   I say amen, Gonzalo.

GONZALO Was Milan thrust from Milan, that his issue
Should become Kings of Naples? O rejoice
Beyond a common joy, and set it down
With gold on lasting pillars. In one voyage
Did Claribel her husband find at Tunis,
And Ferdinand, her brother, found a wife,   210
Where he himself was lost; Prospero, his
    Dukedom
In a poor isle; and all of us, ourselves,
When no man was his own.

ALONSO [*To* FERDINAND *and* MIRANDA] Give me your
    hands;
Let grief and sorrow still embrace his heart
That doth not wish you joy.

GONZALO   Be it so, amen.
Enter ARIEL, *with the* MASTER *and* BOATSWAIN *amazedly*
following
O look, sir, look, sir, here is more of us.

217–18   I . . . drown *See Act one, scene 1, lines 30–31.*

218   Blasphemy *He addresses the blaspheming Boatswain as if he were Blasphemy itself.*

219   That . . . o'erboard *You who swear so much at sea that you drive divine grace from the ship*

223   but . . . since *only three hours ago*
       gave out *declared to be*

224   Is . . . rigged *Is watertight and ready, and as well fitted out*

226   tricksy *neat and pretty*

227–8   strengthen . . . stranger *become more and more strange*

231   clapped . . . hatches *locked beneath the deck*

232   but even *only just*
       several *various*

234   mo diversity *further variety*

236   in . . . trim *perfectly fitted out for sailing*

237–8   our . . . her *and the Master of the ship dancing with joy to see it*

238   on . . . you *in an instant, if you please*

240   moping *stunned, dumbfounded*

241   Diligence *As the Boatswain was Blasphemy itself, so Ariel is Diligence itself.*

242   maze *Alonso compares the baffling complexity of the events with an artificial maze, deliberately constructed for people to lose themselves in.*

243–4   there . . . of *this strange course of events must have been guided by some more than natural power*

245   rectify . . . knowledge *correct our information*

I prophesied, if a gallows were on land
This fellow could not drown. Now, Blasphemy,
That swear'st grace o'erboard, not an oath on
    shore?
Hast thou no mouth by land? What is the news? 220
BOATSWAIN The best news is that we have safely found
Our King and company; the next, our ship,
Which but three glasses since we gave out split,
Is tight and yare, and bravely rigged as when
We first put out to sea.
ARIEL   Sir, all this service
Have I done since I went.
PROSPERO   My tricksy spirit!
ALONSO   These are not natural events, they
    strengthen
From strange to stranger; say, how came you
    hither?
BOATSWAIN If I did think, sir, I were well awake,
I'd strive to tell you. We were dead of sleep,   230
And – how we know not – all clapped under
    hatches,
Where, but even now, with strange and several
    noises
Of roaring, shrieking, howling, jingling chains,
And mo diversity of sounds, all horrible,
We were awaked; straightway, at liberty;
Where we, in all her trim, freshly beheld
Our royal, good, and gallant ship; our Master
Capering to eye her; on a trice, so please you,
Even in a dream, were we divided from them,
And were brought moping hither.
ARIEL   Was't well done? 240
PROSPERO   Bravely, my Diligence; thou shalt be free.
ALONSO   This is as strange a maze as e'er men trod,
And there is in this business more than nature
Was ever conduct of: some oracle
Must rectify our knowledge.

246   infest *trouble*

247–50   at . . . accidents *at a more carefully chosen moment of leisure—and leisure will soon be more continuously available to us—I will explain to you every incident that has occurred, in a way you will find capable of proof*

251   think . . . well *think the best of everything*

255   odd *not accounted for*

256–7   Every . . . himself *Stephano is drunk and says the opposite of what he means, which is:* 'Let every man look after himself, and no man care for the others'.

258   Coragio *Cheer up!*

259   true spies *reliable observers (i.e. his eyes)*

261   Setebos *He swears by his mother's god.*

             brave *fine. (Compare Miranda's similar reaction earlier in the scene. But Caliban assumes that the human beings are spirits called up by Prospero, just as Miranda had done when her father first showed her Ferdinand.)*

262   fine *Because he is now dressed as Duke of Milan.*

265–6   one . . . marketable *This exactly reproduces Trinculo's reactions in act two, scene 2, on first seeing Caliban: that he is a fish, and that money could be made out of him.*

267   badges *Servants wore badges to show whose service they were in; here Prospero is probably referring to the stolen clothes they are wearing, which, whether or not they had real badges on them, were the 'badges' of their villainy.*

270   control the moon *This was traditionally among the powers of witches.*

271   deal . . . power *operate through the objects over which she had command, outside the limits of her personal power*

172

PROSPERO   Sir, my liege,
    Do not infest your mind with beating on
    The strangeness of this business; at picked
        leisure,
    Which shall be shortly single, I'll resolve you,
    Which to you shall seem probable, of every
    These happened accidents; till when, be
        cheerful   250
    And think of each thing well. Come hither,
        spirit;
    Set Caliban and his companions free;
    Untie the spell. How fares my gracious sir?
                              [*Exit* ARIEL
    There are yet missing of your company
    Some few odd lads that you remember not.

Enter ARIEL, *driving in* CALIBAN, STEPHANO, *and*
    TRINCULO, *in their stolen apparel*

STEPHANO Every man shift for all the rest, and let no
    man take care for himself, for all is but Fortune.
    Coragio, bully-monster, coragio!
TRINCULO If these be true spies which I wear in my
    head, here's a goodly sight.   260
CALIBAN   O Setebos, these be brave spirits indeed:
    How fine my master is! I am afraid
    He will chastise me.
SEBASTIAN   Ha, ha!
    What things are these, my lord Anthonio?
    Will money buy 'em?
ANTHONIO   Very like; one of them
    Is a plain fish and no doubt marketable.
PROSPERO Mark but the badges of these men, my lords,
    Then say if they be true. This mis-shapen
        knave,
    His mother was a witch, and one so strong
    That could control the moon, make flows and
        ebbs,   270
    And deal in her command, without her power.

279   reeling ripe *drunk enough to stagger*

280   grand *powerful*
           gilded 'em *flushed their cheeks*
281   How . . . pickle? *A pun: both 'How did you come to be pickled in liquor?' and 'How did you get into this mess?'*
284   I . . . fly-blowing *I shall not be afraid of being corrupted by flies (because he is pickled meat, not fresh).*

289   sore *A pun: both 'bad' and 'smarting'.*
290   This *i.e. Caliban*

294   trim it handsomely *decorate the cell neatly*

296   grace *The main sense of this is 'Prospero's pardon', but we are also free to suppose that Caliban at last intends to seek for divine grace.*

299   luggage *encumbrances (i.e. the clothing)*

These three have robbed me; and this demi-
  devil –
For he's a bastard one – had plotted with them
To take my life. Two of these fellows you
Must know and own; this thing of darkness I
Acknowledge mine.

CALIBAN   I shall be pinched to death.

ALONSO   Is not this Stephano, my drunken butler?

SEBASTIAN   He is drunk now; where had he wine?

ALONSO   And Trinculo is reeling ripe; where should
  they
    Find this grand liquor that hath gilded 'em?   280
    How cam'st thou in this pickle?

TRINCULO   I have been in such a pickle since I saw
  you last that I fear me will never out of my bones.
  I shall not fear fly-blowing.

SEBASTIAN   Why, how now, Stephano?

STEPHANO   O touch me not, I am not Stephano but a
  cramp.

PROSPERO   You'd be king o' th' isle, sirrah?

STEPHANO   I should have been a sore one then.

ALONSO   This is as strange a thing as e'er I looked on. 290

PROSPERO   He is as disproportioned in his manners
    As in his shape. Go sirrah, to my cell;
    Take with you your companions. As you look
    To have my pardon, trim it handsomely.

CALIBAN   Ay, that I will. And I'll be wise hereafter,
    And seek for grace. What a thrice-double ass
    Was I to take this drunkard for a god
    And worship this dull fool!

PROSPERO   Go to, away.

ALONSO   Hence, and bestow your luggage where you
  found it.

SEBASTIAN   Or stole it rather.   300

          [Exeunt CALIBAN, STEPHANO, and TRINCULO

PROSPERO   Sir, I invite your Highness and your train
    To my poor cell, where you shall take your rest

For this one night, which, part of it, I'll waste
With such discourse as I not doubt shall make it
Go quick away: the story of my life
And the particular accidents gone by
Since I came to this isle; and in the morn
I'll bring you to your ship, and so to Naples,
Where I have hope to see the nuptial
Of these our dear-belovèd solemnised,   310
And thence retire me to my Milan, where
Every third thought shall be my grave.

ALONSO   I long
To hear the story of your life, which must
Take the ear strangely.

PROSPERO   I'll deliver all,
And promise you calm seas, auspicious gales,
And sail so expeditious that shall catch
Your royal fleet far off. My Ariel! chick,
That is thy charge; then to the elements
Be free and fare thou well! Please you draw
    near.

                                            [*Exeunt*

EPILOGUE

1   Now . . . o'erthrown *The actor steps partly outside his role to address the audience directly: the powers he possessed as a stage-magician cease to exist as the play comes to its end.*

3   faint *weak*

8   this . . . island *i.e. the stage. At the end of the play, it is the audience who possess magic powers, and can either make or mar an actor's reputation, or a dramatist's.*

9   bands *bondage*

10   With . . . hands *i.e. by clapping the performance*

11   Gentle breath *i.e. cheers, etc.*

12   project *plan, experiment*

13   want *lack*

16   prayer *Both his request for the audience's applause and prayer to God: in its closing lines the speech takes an unexpectedly serious turn.*

17   assaults *makes a violent demand of*

19–20 As . . . free *For the thought of these lines, compare the Lord's Prayer: 'Forgive us our trespasses, as we forgive them that trespass against us'.*

EPILOGUE

Enter PROSPERO

PROSPERO   Now my charms are all o'erthrown,
And what strength I have's mine own,
Which is most faint; now, 'tis true,
I must be here confined by you,
Or sent to Naples. Let me not,
Since I have my Dukedom got,
And pardoned the deceiver, dwell
In this bare island, by your spell;
But release me from my bands
With the help of your good hands.   10
Gentle breath of yours my sails
Must fill, or else my project fails,
Which was to please. Now I want
Spirits to enforce, art to enchant;
And my ending is despair,
Unless I be relieved by prayer,
Which pierces so that it assaults
Mercy itself, and frees all faults.
As you from crimes would pardoned be,
Let your indulgence set me free.   20

[*Exit*

The critic's choice...

MACMILLAN CRITICAL COMMENTARIES
  A series of commentaries on literary classics,
for schools and universities.

The Tempest

John Dixon Hunt

  A clear, incisive commentary providing a
point-by-point analysis of this often very
puzzling play with a refreshing, full and complete account of the ideas and problems
raised by it.

MACMILLAN EDUCATION

Also produced by Macmillan
Shakespeare Interviews

devised, written and directed by Robert Tanitch

Four tapes, each of which contains a brief introduction to one of Shakespeare's most popular plays, followed by a searching interview with the main characters in the play. The actions and motives of the characters, and the conflict and drama of their relationships are revealed through the interviewer's skilful questioning.

Shakespeare Interviews can be enjoyed both at a simple and a sophisticated level. For the student coming to Shakespeare for the first time, these tapes will be invaluable in helping him to overcome the initial language barrier. For the student of Shakespeare at CSE, O and A level who is familiar with the play which he is studying, these tapes offer a stimulating approach, and a springboard for new ideas.

Characters interviewed:
Macbeth: Macbeth, Lady Macbeth
Julius Caesar: Brutus, Cassius, Julius Caesar, Mark Antony
Hamlet: Hamlet, Ophelia, Polonius, Claudius, Gertrude
Romeo and Juliet: Romeo, Juliet, Mercutio, Friar Lawrence, the Nurse.

Macbeth	open reel 333 15111 9	cassette 333 15373 1
Julius Caesar	open reel 333 15112 7	cassette 333 15375 8
Hamlet	open reel 333 15113 5	cassette 333 15376 6
Romeo and Juliet	open reel 333 15114 3	cassette 333 15377 4